AFTER EFFECTS

AFTER EFFECTS

a memoir of
Complicated Grief

ANDREA GILATS

University of Minnesota Press
Minneapolis • London

Published by the University of Minnesota Press
111 Third Avenue South, Suite 290
Minneapolis, MN 55401-2520
http://www.upress.umn.edu

ISBN 978-1-5179-1218-5

A Cataloging-in-Publication record for this book is
available from the Library of Congress. Printed in the
United States of America on acid-free paper

The University of Minnesota is an equal-opportunity
educator and employer.

28 27 26 25 24 23 22 21   10 9 8 7 6 5 4 3 2 1

for Tom Dayton

JULY 10, 1946–JULY 28, 1998

CONTENTS

A Story Untold

MY HUSBAND, Thomas Dayton, died in 1998 at the age of
fifty-two, ending his five-month battle with cancer. As you can
imagine, my life changed dramatically at that point. I grieved
intensely for nearly ten years and lived with unresolved grief
for ten more. During the first two years after Tom's death,
I sustained our marriage by writing him daily letters, but
because my grief was so intense and lasted so long, I could
not bear to look at them until many years later. They rested in
a dusty accordion folder on my closet floor until 2017, when,
after a conversation with a friend, I finally found the courage
to read them. As I made my way through the letters, I began
to realize that they contained the seeds of a potentially meaningful memoir.

We are expected to recover from even our most grievous
losses by traveling a relatively straightforward psychological progression from the actual loss (bereavement), to our
responses to that loss (grief), to learning to live with our loss
(mourning), and to the return to a satisfying life (recovery).

Along this path we might encounter ditches and detours, but experts agree that recovery from acute or "active" grief is as normal as grief itself. But what if we cannot meet this expectation? What if this so-called recovery is somehow disrupted or undermined? What if these "normal" processes take an abnormally long time to take hold? What if they fail us altogether? What if something inside us will not allow us to release ourselves and move forward?

These were the questions bubbling up within me as I immersed myself in writing *After Effects*. As I wrote, I researched, and eventually, quite by chance, I encountered the pioneering work of Dr. M. Katherine Shear, the founder and director of Columbia University's Center for Complicated Grief. In a transformational catharsis, I discovered that for nearly two decades, I had suffered from a known disorder called "complicated grief": acute grief that is abnormally intense and prolonged. Even though complicated grief affects up to one in seven bereaved people, many of them never recognize that the course of their grief is not normal, as I did not, and suffer in silence, as I did.

Shear tells us in her article "Grief and Mourning Gone Awry: Pathway and Course of Complicated Grief" in *Dialogues in Clinical Neuroscience* that complicated grief is a "superimposed process that alters grief and modifies its course for the worse." Grief is considered complicated if it continues to be acute for at least a year after the loss and if the bereaved person is experiencing persistent yearning or longing for the person who has died, a recurring desire to die in order to be reunited with that person, refusal to believe that the grieving person's loved one is really gone forever, inappropriately intense reactions to memories of the person who has died, and "distress or impairment in social, occupational, or other important areas of functioning."

It is one thing to grieve and ultimately recover, but it is another to live in a chronic state of acute grief for nearly twenty years. I never found this experience in my search for books that felt complex and genuine, that would affirm my often-disordered feelings, and that would offer respite as I struggled to live on after Tom's death. In my daily letter to him on December 17, 1998, I wrote:

> It's the ordinary stories that never seem to get told, and the stories that do get told get told because these things have happened to writers. When I was at Barnes & Noble in August looking in the grief and bereavement section—honest to God that's the name of the section—I found absolutely nothing I could relate to. Everything is written either by a psychologist, a physician, a theologian, or some other kind of expert. The only memoirs about these kinds of experiences are written, as I say, by writers.

I confess to being a writer, but I have come only lately to a dedicated writing practice that allows me to mine the vast territory of memoir, a generous form in which it is possible for us to uncover the selves that lie beneath the known self. Once, in a talk, the poet and story writer Grace Paley said that "some people have to live first, then write." I am one of those, and I offer my story of complicated grief to you not only as a writer but as an ordinary someone who has loved, lost, and yet lives.

PART I
DROWNING

I

Into Widowhood

TO MY HORROR, that morning Tom miraculously walked from our bedroom into the living room. Oh my God! What if he fell? Even after losing so much weight, his six-foot-three-inch frame still supported nearly two hundred pounds.

"Where are you going?"

"Porch." (His last word.)

To my relief, he sat down in his easy chair. What was I thinking? Would it really matter if he had fallen? He was hours away from death.

I knew this would be the day. I could tell by studying him. He sat stone-still except for an occasional twitch, his eyes were loosely closed, his skin felt clammy, and his head was covered in sweat. On advice given me a few days earlier by an experienced hospice nurse, I decided to help him along by giving him all the morphine he could take. By then, he could no longer talk, so he could not ask. By then, he could not drink, so I swabbed the red (or was it clear?) liquid along his inner lips, on his tongue, and throughout the inside of his mouth. His breathing was regular; he was calm.

I waited with him. When he had not moved by early afternoon, I decided to risk leaving him to take a shower, my first in four days. I quickly showered. Nothing had changed. But during the ten minutes it took me to dress, he had become more agitated, more restive. I knelt at his knees and began to softly speak to him. Out of the blue, he leaned forward and kissed me hard. (He was always so romantic.) I continued to offer words of love, reassuring him that even if he went, we would never be apart. To my surprise, he brushed his hand across his forehead. Several minutes after that, he stopped breathing. I kept checking, believing his breath would return. It did not. He had died.

*

Five weeks earlier, he had decided to stop treatment. Wasted by cancer, wiped out by chemo, and fried from radiation, he entered home hospice care. During the introductory hospice visit, the supervising nurse gave me a small blue booklet called "Gone from My Sight," the title taken from a Henry Van Dyke poem. On the cover was a line drawing of a tall ship sailing away from the viewer, making for the horizon. The booklet was so simply written and the print so large that at first I turned up my academically trained nose at it. "Show me the research!" I thought, echoing my clarion call of the past five months. But the truth was that I already knew that the research offered no help, and I had never taken care of a terminally ill person, and I had never seen anyone die, and I had never helped anyone die, and I did not know what to do.

To make matters worse, our hospice nurse (whose name I am glad I can't remember) was an uncommunicative, inexperienced fellow who did not visit frequently enough because he misjudged Tom's progress toward death. When he did visit, he seemed unsure of what to say or how to behave. He checked Tom's vital signs, but little else. He kept warning me about all the things I should be afraid of: choking, vomiting, falling, seizure, overdose, fever, bedwetting, and shitting, you name it. Notably, he could not answer my questions about how to dose Tom's medications so that he could feel pain-free and relaxed without sinking into a heavy fog. In such a situation, true answers are nuanced, and this fellow's skills had not reached that level of refinement. Why was I supposed to deny habit-forming drugs to a dying man? What was the point? This nurse's presence was not comforting; it was an irritation in an otherwise temperate day.

No one around us, including our hospice nurse, seemed to understand that Tom was still human, he could still think, he was entitled to both agency and dignity, and he sincerely did not want strangers or even friends taking care of him. He wanted only me, and during that time, I existed only for him, worrying day and night about all those dangerous possibilities, yet never having the presence of mind to step back and consider them in the light of the inevitable and now imminent eventuality: his death.

To compensate for the lack of helpful humans, the humble blue booklet became my bible. It was true that because of my ignorance about death and my rush to judgment, I prematurely and wrongly concluded that the dying experience described in the booklet probably did not apply to Tom because it seemed to refer to an elderly person. But by the time I discarded the booklet a week or two after the funeral, I had come to believe that its content could apply to people of almost any age who are dying of disease. Based on my experience, I can attest that it clearly and accurately laid out the discernible, visible signs on the human journey toward death.

The author of "Gone from My Sight," Barbara Karnes, an internationally famous hospice nurse, lists thirty-two signs to look for in your beloved patient as he or she journeys toward death. She organizes them in four chronological increments: one to three months before death, one to two weeks before death, days or hours before death, and minutes before death. Karnes's signs apply to an aggregate rendered as a typical individual; to express a more specific truth, I must add my own observations to them.

One month before death, he begins to withdraw from the outside world, including extended family and friends. He sleeps more, he no longer enjoys conversation, he loses interest in pastimes like watching television or reading. One week before death, he sleeps most of the day, he eats less frequently and less at a sitting, he alternately feels too hot or too cold, he can no longer laugh, he sometimes feels himself in two separate bodies, one sick and the other healthy, but residing in a different world. Hours before death, he no longer urinates or moves his bowels, his pulse is hard to find, he can no longer keep his eyes open, he cannot close his hand around mine. Minutes before death, the elapsed time between his breaths becomes too long, and he cannot be awakened.

This was the time of truest love. This was the time of absolute devotion. Without reasoning or reckoning or realization, I had laid aside my individuated personhood to become one with him. I was his extended self, the actor on his thoughts, the salve for his feelings, the motor for his body, the executor of his selfhood, his manifest soul. This is the honor of caregiving. This is when the most harrowing experience of one's life also becomes the most precious. Not only was I living for him, I was living as him. I was guarding his life with mine. I was not aware of this at the time; I could not have put it into words. Then, I was only doing what I could.

That is why, as I write today, the gestures of compassion I could have made but did not make continue to torment me. For over twenty years, I have resisted these cruel memories with all my might, but they insist on visiting me, unreconciled and unadulterated, bringing with them waves of guilt so engulfing that they choke me. The most gut-wrenching of them arose from an episode that occurred a few days before Tom began hospice care. At the time, his immune system was severely compromised from chemotherapy and radiation treatments, and the rest of his body was weak from disease. Seemingly out of nowhere, he developed a severe infection. His temperature soared to 104 degrees, and Tylenol did not lower his fever. I called his oncologist, who sent us to the University of Minnesota hospital in Minneapolis, where he was immediately admitted.

There he began an intravenous course of hospital-strength Tylenol along with an antibiotic and a drug designed to quickly reduce his white blood cell count, which had skyrocketed. Within two or three hours, he began to feel a little better, partly because he was more relaxed. Unsurprisingly, that is when boredom and restlessness set in. To combat these irritations, he sent me on several errands: to get the *St. Paul Pioneer Press* (our hometown paper), the Minneapolis *Star Tribune*, and the University of Minnesota *Daily*; to get an Almond Joy; to get a Haralson apple; to get a carton of two-percent milk. After what seemed an interminable wait, his oncologist visited, and after examining the patient, ordered him to spend the night in the hospital. The doctor wanted to give the drugs twenty-four hours to do their work. If, by the following day, Tom's temperature and white blood cell count were normal, he would discharge him.

Afternoon turned to evening. We sat side by side, Tom in his bed and I in an armchair beside it, and ate our hospital dinners. We discussed whether I should spend the night at the hospital or sleep at home and return to the hospital early in the morning. A nearby nurse offered, in passing, to wheel a recliner into Tom's room if I wanted to stay. Characteristically, Tom said the choice was mine, but I knew he wanted me to stay. He was scared, he was sick, and he needed me. I knew that, and I also knew that I would not sleep if I stayed. I was tired to my bones and already worried about taking care of him once he got home. By then, we both knew the end was coming. I loved him absolutely, I was in anguish, but I spent the night at home.

If I were forced to choose one and only one regret over my long life, this would be it. Sleeping at the hospital that night would not have altered the course of Tom's life, but it would have been an act of comfort that, for the smallest of sacrifices, would have brought him the peace he so urgently needed in that lonely, antiseptic place. That I did not give him that small gift, and that his death made it impossible for me to seek his forgiveness, will haunt me to my grave.

*

There was a funeral at Fort Snelling National Cemetery near Minneapolis, the place where Tom, as a U.S. Navy veteran, wanted to be buried, and where I, as his wife, would also be buried. My sister Nan and brother-in-law Allen picked me up, and we drove in silence to the cemetery. Oddly and unforgettably, I found the music playing on their car radio unbearable and asked Allen to turn it off. Nor could I bring myself to converse. As we entered the area where the service was to take place, I wondered aloud whether we were at the wrong funeral. Stretched out alongside us was a seemingly never-ending procession of at least eighty cars and twenty Harley-Davidson motorcycles. (Tom worked at a company that supplied parts to Harley-Davidson.) I had no inkling that the procession would be so long, and because I was so stunned by what I was seeing, this dazzling demonstration of friendship and respect only made me feel worse, as if that were possible.

My family and I settled into the small shelter where the service would be held. The rabbi who performed the service gave me the traditional black *kriah* ribbon that I would pin to my underclothes for the next thirty days. As is customary, I gently tore one end of the ribbon, symbolically performing the ancient Jewish rite of tearing one's clothing as an expression of sorrow. The rabbi offered prayers over Tom's body, and the Jewish mourner's *kaddish* was recited in Hebrew by those who knew it. There was a surprisingly soft seven-gun salute, and I was given the American flag that had been draped over Tom's casket. Taps was blown. After the service, his body was buried, which not only provided me with a place where I could visit him but gave me a sneak peek at my own grave. In fact, a few weeks later, during one of my daily visits, a grounds worker told me that unlike many cemeteries, Fort Snelling did not bury spouses on top of each other, but side by side. He showed me the exact patch of ground into which my grave would be dug.

After the funeral, there was the customary *Seudat Havra'ah* (meal of consolation) at Nan and Allen's home. Traditional postfuneral foods were served: hard-boiled eggs to symbolize new life and bagels to symbolize the unbroken circle of life. After the meal, Tom's and my nephews planted a memorial tree in Nan's backyard. With the funeral behind us, a weekend crammed with family visits ensued. On Monday, the seventh day after Tom's death, everyone except me went back to their usual weekday routines. The flurry of postdeath activity was over, the shock was wearing off, and the numbness in my being was congealing. I was taking five weeks' leave from my job at the University of Minnesota, plenty of time, I imagined, to contemplate whether I would live or die.

*

Too many of us have lived through cataclysmic disruptions in the continuity of our lives. We have had experiences that completely upended us, forcing us to abandon all we took for granted. I think of these disruptions as fissures because they are traumatic in origin, like the opening of a fault line during an earthquake. A fissure puts us abruptly and suddenly in a situation where it is not possible to go on as we were, yet we cannot see a way forward. In an instant, we have lost our moorings; we are no longer anchored to a reality we thought we could rely on.

Going to prison or having one's house carried away by floodwaters opens a fissure in the life of a person who survives this kind of event. So, I believe, does losing a child or surviving the untimely death of a beloved longtime life partner, though in these cases, we not only lose our moorings, we lose ourselves: our identities, the compasses that allow us to navigate life, our North Stars. We continue to breathe, but we have the feeling that we, too, have died. A fissure, while brought on by an external event, is, at its heart, something felt internally.

Your husband is dead and gone. Whatever you thought your life was has vanished. You are stunned, not for a moment, but for weeks and months. You have passed into a fog. Like a deer who knows no better, you are blindsided at every turn in the road. Bereft and adrift, you are no longer capable of discerning what is real. Your yearning for life as it was when you were happy is so penetrating that all you can think to do is go on as you were, robotically making your way through daily routines as you try to replicate life with him, only without him. At certain moments and in certain situations, you may even think you *are* going on as you were, but all too soon you end up conceding that being without him is simply too excruciating to support such a flimsy charade.

My concession came suddenly, out of the blue and through my fog. It happened less than two weeks after Tom's death as I was driving west on Interstate 90 toward the South Dakota state line. Days before he died, we had agreed that "after it was over" I should take a vacation. We had always loved hitting the road, and we thought a road trip might lift my spirits. Even "after it was over," I continued to hope that a journey west, with its breathtaking topographies and novel diversions, would revive me. My sister Resa was living in Denver at the time, and our plan was that I would drive there, and after spending a night with her, she and I would take a three-day trip to Santa Fe, New Mexico, only a day's drive away. On our return, I would spend another night with her in Denver, and from there I would drive home to St. Paul by way of

Deadwood, South Dakota, a town dedicated to helping tourists forget their troubles.

On the appointed morning, which may have been the morning of August 9, 1998, as I loaded the car, locked the house, and pulled away, I must still have been feeling that a trip would take my mind off "things" and I would begin to feel better. I drove southwest out of the Twin Cities toward Mankato, Minnesota, in silence: no CDs, no tapes, no radio. I could no longer bear the sound of music. Following a route that Tom and I had taken a dozen times, I picked up Minnesota Highway 60 at Mankato and drove southwest to Worthington, Minnesota, where I caught westbound Interstate 90. There was a rest stop about twenty miles west of Worthington where Tom and I had always stopped for lunch, so I planned to eat my tuna sandwich there. (I had always made tuna sandwiches for lunch on the first day of our road trips.) Now, sitting alone at "our" picnic table, I was having trouble finishing my sandwich. I had a knot in my throat, my stomach seemed to be upset, and I think I felt mildly nauseated. I dared not take another bite. Though it was a warm, sunny day, I decided to get back into the car.

That was when the floodgates opened. I managed to drive to the rest stop's pet area, which, thank goodness, was empty of pets and their people. There, still in my car, I had my cry. It was long and it would have been loud, too, but I was trying to get through it without being noticed. What could I have been thinking? I had made a foolish, idiotic, dimwitted mistake. Now that I was almost two hundred miles from home, it had finally hit me. We would never take another trip together ever again. In the course of only a morning, I had strayed too far from him. He was home in St. Paul and I was in the middle of nowhere eating a tuna sandwich alone. I desperately wanted to turn around and drive home, back to where I belonged. Back to him.

I had always thought of myself as someone who could recognize and respect her emotions, but now that person seemed to have disappeared into thin air. I was no longer sentient. Apart from my sorrow, I was numb. I had no idea how grief was supposed to feel; the pain I was feeling in those moments came from far beyond my emotional universe. Was it really possible to feel such agony? To feel so utterly forlorn? What kind of abyss was this? How could I go on?

I tried to think. Resa was expecting me, and I knew how disappointed she would be if I aborted my trip. I must have felt that I owed it to her. I must have felt that I owed it to Tom. I dried my eyes, blew my nose, and drove into South Dakota. Two hours later, I crossed the Missouri river at Chamberlain and entered the West. I stayed the night at Al's Oasis Inn, always our favorite motel. The following day I drove to Denver and spent the night with Resa. The next morning, we drove through a hailstorm to Santa Fe. Three days later, we returned to Denver. That evening I called to cancel my reservation at the Deadwood Gulch Resort. In the morning, I said goodbye to Resa and drove back to Al's for another night's stay. The morning after that, I made a beeline for home.

*

Even before I left for my trip, the sympathy cards had begun arriving, and by the time I returned, there was a sizable pile of them on the floor of our screen porch, the landing place of items deposited into the mail slot on our front door. The cards continued to come almost every day for several weeks, and when all was said and done, there were probably close to a hundred of them, although I can no longer remember any one of them. I do remember that their greetings were usually rendered in pastel script, sometimes with pastel flowers in the background, sometimes with blue birds or white angels. The messages fell loosely into three categories: "With sympathy for your loss," "God is with you," and "May your memories ease your loss." God is with me? Really? If that were true, how could this god-awful thing have happened? May my memories ease my loss? Really? My memories are too goddamn painful to even think about, and when they will not stay away, they bring me acute attacks of unbearable grief, sometimes in public places.

At least half the cards contained handwritten notes elaborating on the sender's feelings of sympathy and offering kindhearted reminiscences of Tom. Though I am sure I must have appreciated these writers' thoughtfulness, I can no longer remember the notes themselves. Instead, the "memory" that has stayed with me is the common theme that seemed to run through so many of them: "Thank God it wasn't me." I think of this as "survivor's relief" rather than what psychologists call "survivor's guilt." Some people cloaked this sentiment in sympathy; others, who may have felt both relief and guilt, made offers of help. A few blessedly honest people actually came right out and said how relieved they were that this horrible thing had not happened to them. Even during such a low time, I understood and sympathized with their perfectly natural reactions; I can even imagine that their honesty must have brought a bit of ironic light into my darkness.

With words of empathy, some people wrote or told me about their own grievous losses. Most often, these stories were about the death of an elderly parent (which, for some fortunate people, is their first direct experience with death) or the tragic loss of a friend or relative in the prime of life. One acquaintance said she knew exactly how I felt because she had been through a difficult divorce, and another wrote about the death of her cat. One of our neighbors sent me a check for five dollars. Countless friends, colleagues, and relatives told me, "Your life will be different now." Different? Really? Fuck off! It will be a hell of a lot worse!

In everything, we desperately seek context. We dearly need ways to make sense of what makes no sense to us. The truth is that even by middle age, the events and experiences we have lived through may not provide adequate preparation for responding appropriately when someone we know experiences a tragedy. I cannot count the times I have asked myself, "How could this have happened?" It is an unanswerable question. We can recite and review both the facts and our rationalizations of them until our minds are numb, and we can intellectualize around our feelings until boredom overtakes us, but neither process helps much when we have no choice but to accept what we cannot bring ourselves to accept.

When you buy a sympathy card for someone who has lost her spouse, think about the survivor for whom the card is intended. Choose the greeting with her in mind or buy a blank card and choose your own words as though you were the recipient. Remember that she may be painfully sensitive to any attempt to describe how she must be feeling, even if you, yourself, have experienced a comparable loss. Say instead that you can imagine, that you empathize, that you have her in your thoughts. It may be enough to simply let her know that you are holding her in your heart.

Do not presume that she feels close to God right now. Avoid using neutral words like "different" or "change" to comment on her loss, and for heaven's sake, do not tell her that she is beginning a new journey: such a statement is offensive after a significant loss. Above all, never try to tell her what she already knows: that she feels as if one of her limbs has been amputated, that she cannot focus or concentrate, that she is tired to her soul after five months of deep, tender caregiving, that she has started taking her husband's leftover Ativan so she can sleep alone in her marriage bed, that she has separated from the bustling world and is now a missing person.

2

A Verbatim Experience of Grief

BY TUESDAY, AUGUST 4, 1998, the eighth day after Tom's death, I could no longer endure the silence between us. How can you suddenly stop conversing with the person with whom you talked every day about everything in a relationship in which ongoing dialogue was as essential to your lives as eating and sleeping? Even during times when we were silent, each of us was aware of the other's availability. That is the point. It is one thing to be aware of another person's presence, but for us, it was ontological: we presumed each other's engaged presence as a fact of our lives. An interlude of silence in a lifetime conversation with one's intimate other is a far constellation from the silence of living alone.

Why had I not thought of this sooner? How could I have accepted eternal silence so obediently? But that is the death game. In the blink of an eye, in the split second when death is discerned, all is cut. Next step? Carry on. Seven days of carrying on was enough. I rescinded my acceptance. I decided that I would simply resume talking with him, both aloud and in daily letters, which I faithfully wrote as my first and foremost morning obligation. Even after I returned to work, I continued to put my conversations with Tom first. Only after I had written my daily piece to him did I begin my early morning routine of more writing, this time for my job.

It turned out that I had so much to say that I wrote to Tom for 754 days in a row, writing my final letter on August 26, 2000. For over two years, I wrote and wrote, but I never read. Even when scrolling through the documents into which I typed my letters, I averted my eyes from the text. In 2005, when I converted to a new computer system, I had to copy and paste all 754 letters into new files. But even then, I managed to avert my eyes. As a backup, I also printed every letter. Once again, I did not read the text. I did not even peek. I could not bear to look into the mirror of my grief.

Finally, in April 2017, after almost nineteen years, I looked. I read. I read and read, but not because I wanted to remember. I read in order to consider whether my letters might help others who might be walking a similar path. I read to discover whether my experience of grief was a story: a narrative with a beginning, a middle, and, most important, an end. Surprisingly, I was also curious. Would anything I said still resonate within me? After nineteen years, would I even recognize myself? Would I recognize Tom? Would the unbearable grief I felt then have healed? Would it have found a peaceful resting place in my memory?

As I read, I became transfixed; I felt like someone watching someone else's house burn down. However, I soon discovered that even watching a burning building with its flames and flashes, its ever-changing array of fire colors, and its hisses and bursts, can become flat and monotonous. The mind eventually reads it like a test pattern on a 1950s television: a dreary, unswerving line that moves continually across the screen but never changes its direction, speed, or form. After reading 754 letters, I realized that my experience of grief did not change much over the two years during which I wrote to Tom. Rather than feeling better as time went on, I adapted to a steady state of sadness. Rather than fighting for my own life, I accepted my half-death.

I was fortunate that my job provided continuity: frankly, it was all I had. Still, even at its most meaningful, the work I did was hard. In truth, I always felt that because it centered on human relationships, it pushed uncomfortably against my natural bent toward introversion, but I worked in a humane environment with generous, good-hearted, tolerant people. I was blessed to be part of a supportive gaggle of women colleagues, all doing similar work, all close in age, all feminists. Among them was a gregarious, prodigiously intelligent woman named Carol Daly, my only Jewish colleague. Carol had a happy life because she willed it. Indeed, she was a master at willing to be happy, but her happiness was shattered three months before mine. In a tragic coincidence, Carol's beloved husband, Peter, died of lung cancer on April 23, 1998, at the age of fifty-eight.

Our shared experiences of grief brought Carol and me together, and I often wrote about her to Tom. At the time, it never occurred to me that I was writing two stories in one: Carol's (as I saw it) and mine. Now, so many years later, the chance to read my impressions of another woman's contemporaneous experience of grief has brought startling clarity to my perspective. Carol Daly was a force for optimism to all who knew her, and without her experience to learn from, I would never have recognized that I had been vanquished by sadness. Only now can I see this. In a final irony, Carol died of bile duct cancer on March 6, 2012, at the age of sixty-nine.

*

AUGUST 9, 1998

I seem to have lost my ability to be alone with myself, just doing things that I've always liked to do. I hate thinking because it seems like my mind always goes toward either missing you or painful thoughts of you when you were sick. (At least, thank God, now you're not sick, and I'm so grateful for that.) So I wonder if and when I'll ever become a person who can live in a peaceful, satisfying way without you and pray that will happen. I can't go on forever on a merry-go-round of running around all day to tire myself out so I can sleep at night (even with the Ativan or Xanax) and keep myself distracted so the painful images and thoughts stay away.

AUGUST 11, 1998

Carol says she really doesn't feel that much better after three months and that was sort of depressing, although I know everyone is different. She said that she's really having a hard time concentrating at work and it seems like a chore and she said she feels that she's a lot less efficient and has a harder time getting stuff done. It's really funny because she's always been so enthusiastic about her job and always said she'd be there until she retired. In October, she'll qualify for retirement under the rule of 75 and she's seriously thinking of retiring.

But it's interesting because there are some differences between us, especially in a spiritual sense. She doesn't really believe in heaven or an afterlife and can't bring herself to believe that Peter is waiting for her. At the same time, she told me that she wants her "full measure" of life and wants to go on living. For me, I'm not so sure. If I'm going to live, I really want and desperately need to get to a point where I can make a peaceful, relatively happy life for myself without you, but where I can keep your loving memories with me in a way that will bring me peace and happiness and not such horrible pain.

AUGUST 26, 1998

Honey, it's beginning to dawn on me how much of "me" went with you. I'm probably less than half who I was before you died, so everything is kind of half there or half real.

SEPTEMBER 8, 1998

I still feel your presence in the house. I don't know how to explain it and it would be easy to just say that it's because all your things are here and the memories of you are here, but it's more than that. It's a spirit that makes me feel comforted.

SEPTEMBER 9, 1998

Honey, I'm scared about going back to work because I don't know what my future is there. I must say that I'm tired of the pressures of programming, but maybe it will be different now that I have a new perspective on what's important. It's not that I wouldn't work hard, it's just that I can't take things as much to heart anymore, not after this. It's not a bad feeling to know that nothing worse can happen to you and that even your death will be welcome and something to feel good about it.

SEPTEMBER 18, 1998

I keep comparing myself to Carol—she works a lot, although yesterday I was talking to Claire, this other woman at work, and she said that Carol only works so much because she doesn't want to go home; she needs to be around people all the time. But I'm not like that and I like going home because I know you're here and also because I love our home and it's a comfortable, safe place for me just like it's always been. So I think I need to stop comparing myself to Carol. I like her a lot, but I need to recognize that she's a different person and does things differently. Also, for her it's been three months longer and I think that makes a difference, too.

OCTOBER 4, 1998

The visit with Carol was really wonderful and I want to tell you some more about it. Honey, she's better. When I asked her how she felt compared to two or three months ago, she never came right out and said that she was getting a little better, but in the way she talked about things, I knew it was true. Carol said that she was just letting life happen to her now, which I think is a really good way to put it. If you can't look back and you can't look ahead, you have no choice but to live one day at a time and you know, I still feel this sense of achievement when I put one more day behind me, just that I got through another day no matter how bad a day it was.

OCTOBER 7, 1998

Honey, it's odd how the world can look. First, everybody looks like couples to me—everybody has somebody that they're growing old with and I feel left out and cheated, then I look and I see that there are an incredible number of widows and they look happy and well-adjusted. Older men bother me too; sometimes it's hard for me to look at them— you know, men in their sixties or whatever, and Carol told me the same thing.

OCTOBER 15, 1998

Remember I was telling you about Claire, this woman I work with, who is a very good person but she sometimes speaks before she thinks. I was having lunch with her and Carol yesterday and I was telling them that it was really hard for me when your gravestone came and Carol right away got it because she said was that because of the permanence? And I said, yes, that's a lot of what it's about. And then Claire told us about her mother who was widowed at forty-eight and how she went to the cemetery every day for a year and Claire felt that by doing that she was trapping herself in her grief and preventing herself from going on. So I told them it's restful and comforting to me to go there and be outdoors and just be peaceful with you for a few minutes every day. And then I said to Claire very clearly so that she would understand: "The past is inaccessible to me because it's too painful. The future is unimaginable to me because it's too uncertain and confusing. So I live entirely in the present right now."

NOVEMBER 9, 1998

About my dream. There was a part of it where we were astronauts and we were somewhere for some kind of training. And I don't remember a lot about it except that I was filling out some huge forms that had to be folded many times in order to fit into an envelope and as I was folding this paper, an elderly woman asked me if I was a volunteer and I said, "I'm an astronaut." So then sometime after that we were sitting in some kind of group meeting for astronauts and I was sitting kind of across the room from you and it was a pretty big room with maybe thirty or forty people at this meeting. And I remember thinking how odd our situation was, and the woman who was the leader of the meeting was answering questions. So I asked, if you're married and you thought your husband was dead only it turned out that he wasn't, are you still married? And she kind of joked at my question because it was obvious to her that of course we were still married.

NOVEMBER 13, 1998

Honey, the conflict between not being normal inside and yet having to carry on as though you are is terrible. I feel very very guilty that I'm not earning my keep at work and yet I'm not willing to give up sick time or vacation time right now. I'm thinking that when it's time to do the Split Rock [Arts Program] catalog, I'll have to work overtime so hopefully that will make up for some of it, and truthfully, I have worked so long and hard there over the years, that I'm sure the scales are balanced in my favor. So I think I have to concentrate on just finding ways to get my work done and not worry that I'm not putting in enough time.

NOVEMBER 26, 1998

It's hard for me to imagine living too much longer because half of me is disconnected from my physical life. Half in my body and half with you, so I have a feeling that I won't go on too much longer like this. The part of me that's with you—and really the only access I have to that is when I talk to you and dream about you—is the part that is more me, more whole, more normal, more comfortable in my being. The part of me that's trying to get along in the world is sad and tired and desperate and at sea.

DECEMBER 1, 1998

Honey, Carol is having a bad time. She said that she had a very bad weekend and that she just can't stand to be alone with herself at home. She's very very extroverted and I think needs to be around people a lot, but she said that she used to be perfectly content just staying home with Peter and now she just is constantly looking for something to do and someone to be with. And I really feel for her and I didn't know what to say to comfort her. And she was saying that she's only now realizing that her many women friends, whom she's seen alone for years and years, only want to see her at the times they're not with their husbands. And I totally understand how that goes. She was saying that if she wants to get together with them on Friday or Saturday night, she ends up getting together with them and their husbands and feeling awkward like a third wheel. Boy do I know that feeling.

DECEMBER 2, 1998

I still feel incredibly sad and lonely. And when I say lonely, honey, I mean that in a very specific way. I'm only lonely for you; I only miss you. I hardly ever tell anyone that I'm lonely and I'm very reluctant to use that word because people immediately take it to mean that I need company, any kind of company. And that's not the case at all. I only need you.

DECEMBER 11, 1998

I was thinking that if I were ever to write a guide for a new widow I would definitely tell her to be extremely careful of sympathy cards and not to open them in front of other people and to carefully pick and choose the times when you open them. And especially if you get them at work, don't open them until you get home. People have no idea how hard sympathy cards are; it's a very difficult problem. I could write a whole essay on just that about how other people want to acknowledge, how they want to express, how they want a response because they somehow want to know that even with everything that's happened, you're somehow okay. It's quite amazing. Anyway, I could write an entire treatise just on that. And nowhere in any of the grief stuff I've been reading does it say a word about that or for that matter, about many other things, like those "emotional ambushes."

DECEMBER 12, 1998

I feel good knowing that I finally understand the distinction between missing you and being lonely and that helps me when I have to explain to people. People need things put in the clearest, most basic terms otherwise they won't understand. I wouldn't expect them to understand the meaning of what I'm going through because they haven't experienced it, but I look only for ways to communicate the concept so at least they can figure out how such feelings can be possible.

DECEMBER 17, 1998

I keep thinking about my idea to write out everything that happened from the day you were diagnosed to the day you left your body. And I think too in the back of my mind that I want it all out—out where I can see it in case I do ever decide to write a book. It's the ordinary stories that never seem to get told, and the stories that do get told get told because these things have happened to writers. When I was at Barnes & Noble in August looking in the grief and bereavement section—honest to God honey that's the name of the section—I found absolutely nothing I could relate to. Everything is written either by a psychologist, a physician, a theologian, or some other kind of expert. The memoirs about these kinds of experiences are written, as I say, by writers. The books with life stories in them are mostly about dying and are written by nurses or other helping professionals who work with dying people.

DECEMBER 19, 1998

I sometimes feel that I want to just make a list, a painful, brutal list. No more kissing, no more hugging, no more touching. No more seeing you walk into the living room when you get up on Sunday morning, no more having meals together, no more TV together. No more scratch my back. No more sitting on the floor next to you and leaning against your leg. No more knowing that if there's a blizzard you'll go out into it and get whatever we need. No more driving me anywhere. No more calling me at work. No more trips together, no more going out to eat. No more that you'll carry the grocery bags. No more turkey from the foundry, no more Christmas bonus, no more funny holiday earrings from the lady at the Trend. No more anyone waiting for me to get home, no more anyone caring if I'm late, no more discussions, no more jokes, no more please get me a book if I'm on the toilet, no more couple, no more feeling okay in the world, no more hearing the sound of your voice, no more hearing that I'm cute and pretty, no more burrowing into your back in bed, no more you in bed, no more knowing that someone cares about me more than anyone else in the whole world, no more being first, no more Tom and Andy.

JANUARY 1, 1999

Now I know for sure that Carol is getting better because she told me. She got together the other night with the group of our women colleagues and said that for the first time in four-teen months—since Peter was diagnosed—she felt joy and happiness. What she meant was that she felt the way she used to feel all the time, and she was aware that that was a leap. And she said she's better, honey. And she said I know every-one is different and has a different timeline and there's a dif-ference between eight months and five months, but she said I can see the difference. So I'm very very happy for her honey.

FEBRUARY 15, 1999

I think that to really live, you have to have the context of your life set. You have to make your choices and have a backdrop against which all your joys and interests and other choices are set. And in losing you, I've lost among many other things, that background, that context, that underpinning that would allow me to enjoy everything else in life. Or actually what I mean is to be engaged in the things that people engage in in life. So the things I would normally look forward to, I don't look forward to, and I'm constantly looking for ways to kill time, literally kill time.

FEBRUARY 27, 1999

This business of somehow "making a new life" is for my money some kind of psychological suggestion so that people can get through. The "new life" isn't necessarily a good or happy life and the "new normal" isn't necessarily "right" or peaceful. Yes, people do learn to live with these terrible wounds, but I think that's probably because they don't quite know yet how to die. Or in the case of Carol, she has such a commitment to life that nothing, not even the death of such a beloved person, could shake her from that. But that's not me honey and actually it never was.

MARCH 27, 1999

Anyway, honey, I'm bound and determined to make the list of one hundred things that make me sick at heart and sometimes sick to my stomach, too, just so we'll have it. I may not get up to a hundred, but that's okay, although to be honest it shouldn't be hard at all. I'll just type them in as they come to mind in no particular order.

1. Passing your favorite foods in the grocery store.
2. Not braiding your ponytail anymore.
3. Going anywhere near the hospital and clinics on campus.
4. Not having you call me in the morning.
5. Not having you call me at work.
6. Not being able to hear you say Hi Honey when I come in from work.
7. Not seeing you enjoy your food.
8. Not driving around in the truck.
9. Not going to Annie's Parlor.
10. Not having you drive me to the grocery store.
11. Not having you in the bed at night.
12. Not falling asleep cuddled up against your back.
13. Not being able to hear you tell me you love me.
14. Not being able to hear you tell me I'm cute.
15. Not having my back scratched.
16. All memories of when you were sick. (This one is very very general and I bet I could make a list of one hundred things just within this one area, but it's so painful I couldn't do that right now.)
17. Not hearing you sing in the basement.
18. Not hearing you sing with that funny voice that made me laugh. Especially You'll Never Walk Alone.
19. Not being able to take trips.
20. Not ordering from Waiters.
21. Not eating at the steak house at Mystic.

22. Not being able to take advantage of their all-you-can-eat New York strip sirloin deal for $14.95.
23. Not eating at the Hinckley buffet, my favorite.
24. Not planning trips anymore.
25. Not having you fix things.
26. Not having you stand in the doorway to the bathroom and talk to me while I go.
27. Not seeing your funny hair in the morning.
28. Not having you fling my reading glasses back so you can hug me.
29. Not going shopping together.
30. Not having you to change light bulbs.
31. Not having you to kill spiders.
32. Not watching movies together.
33. Not having discussions about various topics, or more accurately, not being able to hear your opinions when we do have discussions.
34. Not being able to hear your opinions on various decisions about the house.
35. Not being able to see you sitting in your chair.
36. The fact that you never sat in the chair when you weren't sick.
37. Not being able to show you the Split Rock stuff.
38. Not being able to see you lounge on the new couch.
39. Not being able to see you enjoy your truck.
40. Looking at your pictures and having that be too painful.
41. Not being able to look at your pictures.
42. Not seeing, hearing, touching your presence in the house. Just your presence.
43. Not having meals together. Period. All meals.

44. Not shaving your neck.
45. Not filing your corns.
46. Not being able to kiss your forehead.
47. Not having anyone to worry about me.
48. Not being number one to anyone anymore ever again.
49. No sounds in the house when I come in.
50. Not seeing you thump your chest like an ape.
51. The thought of going to any family gathering without you.
52. Any holiday.
53. Not being able to cook foods you like.
54. Seeing your handwriting.
55. Seeing your clothes.
56. Seeing older couples.
57. Seeing older men.
58. Not holding your hand.
59. Not seeing your strawberry fruit bar sticks in the waste basket.
60. Not hearing you say I was ready to call out the dogs if I come in late from work.
61. Going different places and not having anyone in the whole world know or care where I am.
62. Not having anyone in the family ever let me know that they are thinking about you, except Resa.
63. Not having anyone in the family ever even mention you, except Resa.
64. Not having anyone in the family ever go to the cemetery.
65. Knowing you're not sleeping in the bedroom right now.
66. Losing all sense of normalcy or rightness.
67. Being detached from the everyday world.

68. Not being able to hear you when I talk to you about different things.
69. Not sitting on the porch with you.
70. Never again feeling happy on our birthdays.
71. Never again having a happy wedding anniversary.
72. Never feeling complete.
73. Never seeing the bizarre hairstyles you used to make when you'd get out of the shower to make me laugh.
74. Never being able to enjoy music again.
75. Having to avoid music all the time.
76. Never being able to listen to the doo wop tapes again.
77. Never being the object of your affection.
78. Feeling sick if I run into somebody I know.
79. Having to avoid certain places for fear of feeling sick.
80. Not sitting on the porch together.
81. Crying all the time for so long.
82. Getting rid of things that we would never have gotten rid of if this hadn't happened.
83. Cleaning the basement.
84. Never taking joy from anything in life.
85. Not being able to feel other people's joy.
86. Never hearing about the foundry guys anymore.
87. Not seeing the various strange things you brought home from hiking.
88. Looking out the back window and never seeing your truck.
89. Selling your truck.
90. Not having anyone understand the tremendous scope and deep pain of dismantling a material life. It takes months—maybe years—and consists of hundreds of painful activities, each one horribly draining.

91. Not having anyone understand why I'm exhausted. See #90 above.
92. Completely losing my desire to see new places.
93. Remembering your cute little nose on such a big body.
94. Having to keep my relationship with you to myself because you're supposed to be "gone."
95. Being reminded that other people have it worse than me.
96. Not feeling safe in the night like I used to.
97. Having the house so silent when I come home.
98. Feeling pressure from people to "get better" or "get used to it." It incenses me.
99. Not having your creativity and cleverness to make me happy.
100. People thinking that any kind of company can substitute for you.

APRIL 17, 1999

I think about Peter's one-year day coming up on the twenty-third all the time and now I've decided to send Carol flowers and I'll write out a nice note when I get them and I don't really care how much they cost honey because Carol has done so many kind and generous things for me.

APRIL 20, 1999

I'm dead honey. I died with you. The essence of me went with you and in a way, I'm glad you took me along because I think that's the source of our continuing relationship. But I'm trapped here in my body and in a constant state of conflict. I'm not really connected to life and yet I'm not free of my body either.

APRIL 26, 1999

I still can't get over it, honey, how people think they know what's best for me. And the interesting twist to it is that when you were here, I had impunity. Nobody cared what I did or how much I got out, nobody had advice on what's good for me, people seemed to think I was fine, they let me be. They let us be. Now I'm everybody's business. I should be getting out more, I should be joining groups, I should be taking tai chi, I should, apparently, be doing everything except what I'm doing. The funny thing is that people never actually ask what I do with my days; they somehow assume I'm doing absolutely nothing.

MAY 8, 1999

I have felt acutely this "partner privilege" stuff for all these months but I hadn't really crystalized it or given it a name until yesterday. It could apply to a man and woman or two women or two men, but of course my perspective on it is of a woman whose husband has died. And honey I'm aware in a kind of selfish, almost self-pitying way of all the comforts I've lost. I guess I've been afraid to think about it too much or talk about it because it sounds like self-pity but more than that I think I've felt guilty for pitying myself over things that some women never have, in other words, unearned partnership privilege.

Truthfully, I grieve the loss of the partner privileges. You who knows how to rig the curtain rod so it doesn't bow in the middle. You who knows where to plug in the dehumidifier. You who knows how to take the hose off the tub faucet in the basement and attach it to the dehumidifier. You who can change a light bulb or take off a fixture without standing on a chair. You who can listen to the furnace and tell if it's okay. You who can change the furnace filters. You who can talk to workmen and know if things are getting done right. You who can fix a toilet. You who can change a fuse. You who can put new wipers on my car. You who can spot a low tire and listen to the car and know if it's running right. You who made me feel secure because I had a partner. You who could have easily bested any intruder into the house and I always chuckled to myself thinking of any poor fool who would try to break into Tom Dayton's house.

MAY 19, 1999

I look at Carol and realize how much better she's doing. I don't know how she keeps the pace she does, but I'm sure she's always done that to some extent. And I've always kept to myself with you. It's very different—two very different people in many ways with very similar circumstances and very similar feelings except I think mine are more extreme. I think however painful it is, Carol is somehow determined to make her way and I see no way to make mine. I'm not at all saying that my pain is worse than hers or that she has certain advantages or blessings that I don't have, but only how individualized all this is.

MAY 28, 1999

Another 28th honey. The tenth one. Ten months. It never ends. Now that I'm reading all the grief books, it seems like everyone eventually does "get over it." I think this is because the people who don't get over it don't write books.

JUNE 23, 1999

Today is the one-year day of when Dr. Gaffney told us "it's a matter of a few weeks." I don't know what else I can say about it honey. I hate to think about it. Other than you and I, nobody else is aware of it. This is the bad time, the suffering. I push it out of my mind and I can't forget it, I can't forget it. And it literally eats me alive.

JUNE 28, 1999

Now I realize how much time I spent thinking about you each and every day. It's what I said yesterday—it was living my life in consideration of you. Your needs and comforts and preferences and pleasures. And I know you did the same. I end up with a hole in my head, a void, and it ends up getting filled with planning out my chores, speculation about what the neighbors are up to, and a bunch of other crap. I don't feel productive, I don't feel creative, I don't feel engaged, I don't feel anything like me.

JULY 1, 1999

I don't want to forget to tell you about the dream I had. The part I remember is that I was sitting in the living room and you came home and I could see you at the back door from the living room (which is strange because you can't see the back door from where I sit on the couch). But anyway I did and you had a big box that you were carrying so I rushed and opened the door for you. You were coming home from work, I'm sure. But anyway, as soon as I did that somehow the scene shifted and we were in the garage and you had brought home some kind of big box but also a huge dog that had a beautiful reddish brown coat and was some kind of lab or whatever. Very very large. And I think it was a dog that you were taking care of for someone and we were kind of amazed because the dog was lifting some sheets of wall board out of the garage with his two front legs—using them like arms, you know? And we were saying wow, this dog is amazing.

JULY 24, 1999

Honey, I was talking to Carol yesterday about the amazing overuse and misuse of that word "work." It bugs the hell of out of me. The work of grieving. I hate that. I don't know what it means. It's ridiculous to hear people say and read in books that you need to "work through" your grief, or "work on" your healing, etc. For one thing, I'm already so drained from the weight of it that the thought of any more work is repugnant to me. I go to work every day at the University and that's enough. I don't want to feel that I've constantly got to do more work so I'll be . . . what? Emotionally healthy? Happy? (If anybody told me I'd be happy after doing what-ever it is they mean by work, I would know immediately that they had no scruples at all.) When you're grieving you don't have a goal. You don't go through it in order to get better, to achieve something at the other end, if in fact there is an other end, which I'm not convinced there is. Work to me means that you have a goal—to make something, to earn a living, to be productive and engaged. The goal can be the work itself or the outcome of the work, but grieving isn't work. If it were, maybe I wouldn't mind it.

JULY 28, 1999

This is the one-year day honey and I don't know what it means exactly. How many times have I asked what does it mean?

AUGUST 15, 1999

Now I think I'll just admit whenever people intimate that I've changed that I have. People don't like that thought— they don't like to think that someone has changed so much, they don't like to see that the person they knew isn't recognizable to them anymore.

AUGUST 31, 1999

I don't expect much from this life now, I don't expect to be happy or to enjoy myself, I ask very little from this life. I enjoyed sitting and knitting and watching the old movies yesterday morning—that's a perfect example of all I expect. Whatever happiness was before—and I do remember the feeling honey, the idea that it was a foundation for living— it is gone and irretrievable. And I've heard people say and I've read that you replace what you had before with other things—you invent a new life, a new you. Bullshit. You simply pass time. You do what is most pleasant in order to avoid more pain.

SEPTEMBER 3, 1999

There's definitely much more of a difference between me and Carol as time goes on. Carol says she's okay and she means it. She really is. And she's been clear within herself from the day that Peter died that she wants to live. She's certain. What a difference that makes. And she said that as time went on and Peter's hearing became more and more of a problem, they spent less and less time together and her friends became more the center of her life in terms of people to do things with. Which isn't at all to say that she and Pete weren't deeply, deeply connected because they were. But Carol and I are having different experiences at this point—she's better and I'm not. To the point where I feel less comfortable talking with her about it because I'm worried that she'll think I'm off my rocker.

DECEMBER 31, 1999

This is the last day of the year and the century and the millennium. Not that it means anything—I think it doesn't mean a thing actually. As long as I'm tired by tonight and fall asleep early I'll be satisfied. Then it'll all be over. As the song goes, ain't it a kick in the head? Actually it's more like a bomb to the mind.

JANUARY 3, 2000

I think I have a problem with work honey. I don't like going to work anymore. I don't mind the work, I just hate going there, and that's not good. I'm just hoping things will get better. This is the worst I can remember—I haven't ever felt quite like this before—it's different than just being under pressure because of too much work, although if I weren't under this pressure, it might very well be that the other stuff wouldn't seem as bad either.

MARCH 19, 2000

I don't feel like I'm in my mid-fifties. I feel like I'm in my mid-seventies. I look back on my life and I've done everything I could. It doesn't make me sad to think this, and I have absolutely no thought of missing out on anything.

MAY 28, 2000

It's the 28th honey. One year and ten months today. Mostly it seems like forever. Sometimes it seems like a flash, but not so often.

I have to tell you that I had this dream about a little man and his name was Swami Andy. And he was a fully developed man except that he was tiny, about the size of a baby except that he could walk and was an adult. And every time he showed up everyone would pick him up and be very happy to see him, including me. He always wore a little white suit with a vest.

JULY 27, 2000

I think it's life out of balance. Living without a partner. I think it's not a natural way to live even though I know there are single people who are content in their lifestyles. And if you can't be here in your body, I would much rather live alone until I can go to be with you. That's what I was thinking about Carol switching her wedding ring from her left hand to her right hand. That she simply replaces one kind of longing with another. Maybe that's not a kind way to look at it. I hope that if she wants a partner or a companion that she finds one, and usually people do if they want to.

JULY 28, 2000

Well anyway honey today is a heavy day. The two-year day. I don't know if I can talk about it. I don't know what grief is and when it starts and when it finishes.

3

Get Over It or Get Sick

WHEN I RETURNED TO MY JOB on September 14, 1998, I somehow expected that each day I would feel better than the day before, and that after a few months or perhaps a year, I would somehow be myself again. Little did I know that I would be locked inside a penitentiary of intense grief for the next ten years. Already, my prison was escape-proof and enveloping: the thick walls were opaque and soundproof, and my cell contained no windows. The only light was artificial. Somewhere, there must have been a key, but I never thought to look for it.

I had lost my ability to think. I could not bear to think about my beloved Tom, my rock for twenty years. I could not bear to listen to music, which had been my lifeboat since I first heard "The Sicilian Tarantella" on my grandparents' Victrola as a small child. I could no longer bear to paint, my vocation since the age of one. I packed up our stereo equipment and stored it in the basement. I gave my easel, which had been with me since 1974, to my friend Sherry. All my life I had relied on three saving graces: music, painting, and reading. Now, without so much as a second thought, I had abandoned two of them at a time when I most needed saving. And the third was in danger: I could not focus my mind long enough to read a chapter, let alone an entire book.

I could not bear life. I wanted to fall into a deep sleep, perhaps via some kind of inoculation, and stay there until it was over, whether that was months, years, decades, or forever. Though I could not have found these words at the time, I would now define "it" not as my life but as unbearable grief, which, in turn, I would define as an agonizing, insatiable longing for Tom. I had had toothaches, bee stings, and blistering sunburns; I had had influenza, the vomiting flu, and, as a four-year-old, a burning ear infection. I had had my heart broken more than once, but I had never felt pain, whether physical or emotional, that was so excruciating I could not bear it. Yet it was real. There I was, feeling that I would either explode or implode virtually every minute of every day, and there was no respite, there was no relief, there was no one to rescue me. How long could this go on? How could anyone live like this? I had read Elisabeth Kübler-Ross's *On Death and Dying* during Tom's illness, and I had believed her when she said that we are never given more than we can bear. Now I felt mortally betrayed.

I felt finished. I felt that I had done everything I was meant to in this life, and I had convinced myself that I was satisfied with what I had done. I had even had a rational conversation with myself about it. Feeling finished, I concluded, constituted ethical justification in case I decided to commit suicide. For fifty-three years, I had dutifully paid rent on the space I occupied in the world, and I was now entitled to leave guilt-free. It was easy reasoning: I simply preferred being with Tom to living without him. I only remained noncommittal because of the hurt it would cause my family, especially my parents.

The harder part was that I was still alive, I was only fifty-three, I had a mortgage, and I was no longer half of a two-income family. I needed my job in order to survive. The fact that I no longer felt able to carry out my work was beside the point. At least my employer thought so: the University allowed me five days "bereavement leave" to "attend funeral services, ceremonies, and interment, and make necessary arrangements." With my supervisor's permission, I was also eligible to extend my leave by taking unpaid time off or using earned vacation time, which I did for four weeks. The University must have assumed that life and business must go on as usual: employees should do their grieving while working, or better, after hours, a policy that harked back to a time at the turn of the twentieth century when the death rate was double what it was at the turn of the twenty-first century. Pay the price if you have it, or get over it in five days.

Twenty years earlier, sporting a new bachelor of fine arts degree in drawing and painting from the University of Minnesota, I had landed a job at the University as a secretary in a small department called Continuing Education in the Arts. After eleven years working at an insurance company (where many of my workmates thought Jews had horns, largely because they had never known one), this was a dream come true. I knew that I could no longer work in the for-profit world, and I wanted to work in an environment in which I could be close to the arts. Above all, I wanted to serve the arts, to give all I could to this cardinal human endeavor.

By the time I lost Tom, I had served the University for
twenty years. For fifteen of them, I had been directing the Split
Rock Arts Program, a summer series of residential workshops
in the visual and literary arts held at the University's Duluth
campus, just up the hill from Lake Superior. I had cofounded
Split Rock with my then supervisor, who, with the support
of the University's large, well-funded continuing education
unit, was able to give me a free hand. Needless to say, I went
to town. My extraordinarily committed staff and I brought
renowned artists and writers from around the country and the
world to teach in Duluth. All we asked was that they pass on
their gifts, which they did with generosity and virtuosity. Our
students, self-defined artists from all walks of life, came from
every state in the Union, from Canada, and from overseas,
and included people from eighteen to ninety years old.

Split Rock became one of the most respected and sought-
after arts programs in the country, not because its teachers
were famous (even though some were), not because its students were dedicated (even though all were), not because
you could walk down the hill to Lake Superior (even though
you could), but because the program was dedicated to the
proposition that all humans are creative, that each of us has
the inborn capacity to express ourselves in the world and
thereby make our unique mark on that world, not by force
or discipline, not by sacrifice, but by our insistent instinct
for creating and building and inventing and connecting, no
matter the form.

In his landmark 1979 book *The Gift: Imagination and
the Erotic Life of Property*, the poet and essayist Lewis Hyde
brilliantly makes a case that a work of art is a gift, not a
commodity. It circulates in a gift economy, enriching all who

experience it. From the moment I read, in the middle 1980s, the following quote from *The Gift*, I had no doubt about the authority of art. I felt with utter certainty that it was a force of life:

> As is the case with any other circulation of gifts, the commerce of art draws each of its participants into a wider self. The creative spirit moves in a body or ego larger than that of any single person. Works of art are drawn from, and their bestowal nourishes, those parts of our being that are not entirely personal, parts that derive from nature, from the group and the [human] race, from history and tradition, and from the spiritual world. In the realized gifts of the gifted we may taste that *zoë*-life which shall not perish even though each of us, and each generation, shall perish.

I expressed this belief not through my own art but through my unwavering commitment to the Split Rock Arts Program. My colleagues used to joke that Split Rock was my "brainchild," and in a perverse way, that was true. As I went, so went the program. If I had no energy, the program would have no energy. If I were lazy, the program would become smaller and less interesting. If I did not spend enough time, if I did not give enough, the program would not boast the diverse array of teaching artists and workshop topics that our audiences had come to expect. When I returned to my job after Tom died, feeling spent and tired and having no means of recapturing the inner energy that had nourished Split Rock for so long, I was afraid. I was afraid that I would end up killing my brainchild.

For the first time in my University career, I knew what it was like to mark time at a job: to feel disengaged from meaningful work that I was privileged to be able to do, to dread

going to work each morning, to constantly worry that I was
not earning my salary, to become a clock watcher. My workplace existence became more like my homeplace existence:
a rote exercise in killing time. All I wanted was to be left
alone in our home, where I could keep the blinds drawn day
and night, where I could mope to my heart's content, where
I could cry out loud anytime I felt like it, and where I could
smoke as many cigarettes as I wanted.

*

When the spirit is unwilling, the body will follow suit. Even
with a smoking habit, I had always been plump, but I had
steadily lost weight during Tom's illness. I had little or no
appetite and could not always keep my food down. Eating a
favorite meal did not seem to make a difference. If I was eating with family or friends, I was usually able to keep my nausea at bay, but if I was eating alone, as I did most evenings, it
was a crapshoot. Once I had heaved my dinner, my appetite
seemed to diminish even more. I seemed not to be able to feel
physical hunger, and my sensual attraction to food, which
had been both a pleasure and a nemesis all my life, seemed to
have left me when Tom died. I used to tell myself (but no one
else) a sardonic joke: if you want to lose weight, just have
your husband get sick and die.

During the five months between his diagnosis and his
death, Tom lost nearly fifty pounds. I, the "well" one of the
two of us, lost over twenty pounds. But that was just the tip
of my iceberg. Over seven years, from 1998 to 2005, I lost
a third of my body weight, almost fifty pounds, but not by
exerting self-control, since I had none. Even during my most
intense periods of grief, when I suffered almost daily nausea,

I willfully ate fattening, unhealthy foods every chance I got. It was just one of my many grief-driven acts of self-destruction: I must have been trying to convince myself that I still craved junk food, even though my thinning body rebuffed the French fries and pizza I fed it. At the same time, the off-and-on diarrhea I had lived with for most of my life seemed suddenly to be worsening. Unaware and apathetic, I was sliding toward malnutrition and even, perhaps, starvation.

Now I can see that when Tom died, leaving me stranded and unattended in a deep, dark well of grief, I lost the part of myself that knew how to exit the transactional trolley of daily life in order to take a step back and observe myself, and then to take a second step back in order to reflect and analyze. Why could I not eat? Why did I feel such extreme fatigue every single day? Why could I not concentrate long enough to make a grocery list? Why did I feel so utterly disassociated from all the "life" surrounding me? Tom was gone from my sight and I knew what constant sorrow was, but I never thought to wonder about these other changes, even though they were ruling my life. I had detached from my self-consciousness. Not only was I numb, I was blind, deaf, and mute.

Had I thought to look into it, I would have learned that losing a close loved one is a singularly powerful source of stress, and stress can weaken the immune system. So while grief is not normally viewed as an illness unto itself—after all, losing our loved ones is an inevitable part of the human life cycle—it can make us physically sick. While grieving, we are more likely to catch colds, have our colds degrade into pneumonia, be plagued with insomnia when we most need to maintain our meager energy, and suffer from anxiety that leaves us short of breath, which makes us feel panic, which makes our hearts beat too fast, which makes us feel fear. There is even a condition called broken heart syndrome whose symptoms mimic those of a heart attack, but without permanent cardiovascular damage. Related to broken heart syndrome is the "widowhood effect" that most commonly affects older couples and is realized when one spouse dies within months of the other. Researchers attribute this to the fact that grief causes inflammation levels in the body to rise, leading to (actual) heart attacks, strokes, and diseases like cancer that result in premature death.

As if physical symptoms were not enough, losing a spouse also causes an abrupt, rapid descent into loneliness. "Close relationships help regulate our daily psychological and physical functioning, and that loss typically leaves people feeling out of control and disoriented," says Dr. M. Katherine Shear, professor of psychiatry at Columbia University and director of Columbia's Center for Complicated Grief. Shear adds that grief also affects cognition: "It can interfere with the ability to think clearly, to make decisions and judgments, and problem solve." If we cannot think clearly, if we cannot make judgments and solve problems, and if, in this confused state that feels as though it will never ease, we can no longer find a reason to live, what resources are left to keep us from destroying ourselves? None, at least not during the most acute throes of grief. If one is willing to be patient or feels incapable of decisive, intentional action, there are myriad ways to kill oneself without committing suicide. In truth, some of us are already hard at it: we eat ourselves into obesity, we drink alcoholic beverages to excess, and we smoke cigarettes. I was hard at it with a two-pack-a-day habit that voraciously fed my grief.

"If I had to make a choice," I used to tell my girlhood friend

Sherry, "I would rather smoke than eat." It was Sherry who taught me how to smoke. In fact, Sherry taught me everything I knew about the wicked side of teen life: the secret desires of boys, sexual positions and techniques, how to choose uplifting, seductive undergarments, the need to carry condoms in one's handbag, and the proper application of eyeliner so that one looked sultry but not slutty. Even as a teenager, Sherry believed that there was no reason why a girl should not have protected "fun" before marriage. She was the most worldly of the girls in our crowd: she could hold a cigarette in each hand, take a drag from both at the same time, and exhale out of both nostrils simultaneously. She could drag race her father's white Chevy Impala and not get beat or caught, and she had been valedictorian of her middle school class.

During the summer before our junior year in high school, Sherry and I spent a few days with my grandparents at their rental cabin at Paradise Resort on Chisago Lake near Lindstrom, Minnesota, just thirty-eight miles north of St. Paul. Sherry had a daring plan for our vacation: we would practice smoking. To equip ourselves, we each stole a pack of cigarettes from the cartons our mothers kept on hand. (Mine were Tareytons and Sherry's were Marlboros.) We commandeered some matches, and we were ready. Granny and Grandpa's cabin came with a rowboat, which was the linchpin that rendered Sherry's plan feasible. Sherry had learned to row two years earlier, when we were both members of Young Judaea, a Zionist cultural organization for Jewish youth. Young Judaea held summer retreats at Camp Owendigo on Carver Lake, located on what were then the outskirts of St. Paul. The retreats always included recreational activities, from swimming and rowing to hiking and volleyball. Sherry, who was already a good swimmer, learned to row, and I, who lacked any aptitude for outdoor activities, learned to play volleyball.

The plan was that Sherry would row us out to the middle of Chisago Lake, beyond sight of anyone onshore. Once there, we would drop anchor and practice smoking. Our execution was perfect. No one could see us light up (or tear up when the smoke hit our eyes) or hear us cough when we tried to inhale and exhale. We hacked bloody murder, almost passing out and retching overboard during our first few attempts, but our desire to be cool was greater than our bodies' intelligent resistance to tobacco smoke. After two or three cigarettes and an hour or so, the headache, lightheadedness, and sore throat passed, and we were puffing away like Bette Davis in *Now, Voyager*.

At fifteen years old, I would have never dreamed that Sherry's and my rowboat excursion would constitute a turning point in my life, nor, obviously, would I have seen it for the colossally stupid act it was. In 1961, five years before health warnings began appearing on cigarette packs, powerful tobacco companies were actively working to hide a rapidly growing body of research on the destructive effects of cigarette smoking on human health. Although our parents, who themselves were smokers, had half-heartedly told us that smoking was bad for us, we ignored them, just as they had undoubtedly ignored the same advice from their parents. Both my parents quit smoking later in their lives, but despite doing so, both died of and with smoking-related diseases.

*

Though they never confronted me, I knew that my family members, especially my mother, were distraught that I continued to smoke after Tom's death. On the night she died, my mother had a few moments during which she spoke ramblingly but urgently from her deathbed to no one in particular. Still, I am utterly certain that during this morphine-induced babbling, I heard her imploring me to please, please quit smoking. She did not say my name; she referred to me as "she," and though her speech was not lucid, I knew that was her message. I felt ashamed, the same shame I felt with every cigarette I had smoked since Tom's death, and hoped that my siblings did not interpret her words as I did, or did not interpret them at all.

During the decade that my parents owned a grocery store, they both worked every night. My father left for the store early each morning, came home for dinner in the late afternoon, and left again with my mother to work until nine o'clock at night, when the store closed. This was my mother's life: after working in her home from early morning to early evening, she served her family dinner, doled out childcare assignments to her older daughters, and went back to work. My father's life was not much easier: he spent fifteen hours a day at the store.

After the store went bankrupt, Mom worked long hours at an assortment of jobs, including bagging clothes at a neighborhood dry cleaner and selling magazine subscriptions over the telephone. Eventually, she landed a position as bookkeeper at Snyder Drug, a nine-to-five job that suited her talent for working with numbers. By the time she retired from Snyder's, she already had emphysema, a chronic disease caused by smoking and characterized by weakened and ruptured air sacs (called alveoli) in the lungs that make it difficult to inhale and exhale, resulting in shortness of breath. That word was not used, nor was the umbrella acronym COPD (which stands for chronic obstructive pulmonary disease and includes both emphysema and chronic bronchitis). All we knew was that her lungs were diseased and her endurance was diminishing.

Our entire family began pressuring her to quit smoking, and though she tried a couple of times, she fell off the wagon after a day or two. Her heart was not in it. Finally, after being hospitalized for an acute COPD exacerbation (a worsening of symptoms that can last from several days to several weeks and requires treatment with steroids, antibiotics, or both), she managed to quit permanently, but she never stopped resenting the fact that she could no longer smoke, and I can still hear her saying, "For two cents, I would start smoking again." With the help of pulmonary rehabilitation and inhaled and oral steroids, she was able to enjoy life during her seventies, volunteering at Planned Parenthood, taking jaunts to a local casino to play bingo, whupping my father at Scrabble almost every night, and pursuing her lifelong hobby of knitting, at which she was a master.

Her good years would not last. In 2002, two years before she died and twelve years after she quit smoking, Mom caught what she called "the cold of the century." By this time she was rail thin and observably frail. She had no fat reserves, and her strength had been slowly but steadily waning for years. The "cold of the century" not only spawned pneumonia but led to a severe COPD exacerbation that once again put her in the hospital, this time for a longer stay. Early in the morning after she was admitted, I called the nurses' station in her unit to ask how she was feeling. The answering nurse did not mince words: "She's in duress. You should come right away."

I brushed my teeth, dressed, and raced to the hospital. When I entered her room, she was lying on her back gasping for breath, gasping for breath, gasping for breath. Her pulmonologist, Dr. James Flink, whom I credit with saving her life, was standing over her, watching her every breath and occasionally whispering in her ear. (Mom had lost her hearing by then.) When I said hello and took her hand, she murmured, "I didn't want her to see me like this." Thankfully, within a few minutes the medication Dr. Flink had administered began to do its work, and though weary and weak, Mom began to breathe normally. At that point, I (like to) think she was happy to see me, but I was shaken. As soon as my siblings arrived, I snuck out for a cigarette.

After being released from the hospital, Mom spent six weeks recuperating in the transitional care unit at Sholom Home, our local community's Jewish nursing home. That care included muscle strengthening and occupational therapy and was necessary because severe COPD exacerbations like my mother's have lasting effects. While patients do recover from them, they often do not regain the level of lung function they enjoyed before the exacerbation. From this point on, Mom would need round-the-clock oxygen to augment her daily oral prednisone and nebulizer treatments. Nebulizers are the foot soldiers of COPD care because they convert liquid medicine into a mist that is inhaled by breathing normally through a mouthpiece. This allows people who cannot inhale deeply enough to benefit from an inhaler to take bronchodilators and other medications that work in the lungs. For my mother, the nebulizer was a godsend: I am certain it prolonged her life.

My father refused to believe that Mom was dying until the day she died. During the days and weeks after her death, when we tried to ask him how he was feeling, he simply and unsurprisingly said it was better not to think about it. He had had surgery for lung cancer at seventy-seven, from which he fully recovered without the need for chemotherapy. In addition to chronic bronchitis, he had severe edema in his legs, type 2 diabetes, and high blood pressure. His doctors and nurses marveled at him because they could not understand how anyone with that many "conditions" could continue to live. After my mother's death, he suffered from worsening dementia, and about two years before his death, he admitted as much to me, saying, "My memory is shot. I'll have to go to Sholom." Miraculously, he lived to be ninety-three, dying at Sholom in 2009. Medically, my father may have been a paradox, but after my mother died, he told us that he would "hang around as long as I'm interested," and that is exactly what he did.

*

When Tom and I reached our fifties, we talked about trying to quit smoking, but neither of our hearts was in it. We used to rationalize our inaction by asserting that the time was not right: we were under too much stress at work, we were afraid of gaining (more) weight, we would wait to decide until after we returned from our vacation. But the truth was simple and timeless: we were deathly afraid of never being able to smoke again. We were so afraid that nothing, no matter how distressing or tragic or calamitous, could impel us to face that fear. Let me now speak only for myself. How could I have continued to smoke after my own mother died of emphysema? How could I have continued to smoke after my own father was diagnosed with lung cancer? How could I have continued to smoke after my own husband died of "adenocarcinoma of unknown primary"? I had no answers then, and I have no answers now.

After Tom's cancer diagnosis, his attitude about smoking became fatalistically cavalier. He never considered that if he quit smoking, he might save himself, and knowing that his prognosis was grim, I made no effort to convince him to do that. He was suffering enough. Still, rather than feeling afraid, he felt liberated. "I'm going to smoke as much as I want since I'm going to die anyway," he announced, and he was true to his word. During his first chemotherapy treatment, he felt like having a cigarette, so he wheeled his IV pole to the elevator, descended to the first floor of the clinic, wheeled through its busy lobby, and exited through the revolving door to the sidewalk. He then stood and smoked a cigarette, smiling all the while at his paradoxical performance as the chemo cocktail continued to drip from its bag and passersby stared and shook their heads.

That anyone, including me, should or could have expected me to quit smoking while grieving so acutely seemed cruel to me at the time. My previous rationalizations for not quitting were measly compared to this. Finally, I had been given the rationalization to beat all rationalizations. How could I possibly quit smoking when my beloved husband, the heart of my life, had been taken from my sight forever? Grief is predicated on finality: "I will *never* see him again." It was "never" that kept me in acute grief for a decade. Quitting smoking is also predicated on finality: "I can *never* have another cigarette again." It was the combination of these two "nevers" that kept me from giving up smoking for eight years after Tom died. Then, within months of each other, three seemingly unrelated events occurred that, taken together, made it possible for me to quit.

First. In the summer of 2006, I suffered my first COPD

exacerbation. I had been on vacation with my siblings in Las Vegas, where I had caught a doozy of a cold. By the time I deplaned in the Twin Cities, I could hardly stand up, let alone walk. But I made it home, and somehow I must have managed to get through the night. The next morning, I must have gotten out of bed and settled myself on the sofa, because that is where I was when my sister Nan called. I remember staring at the phone as it rang, feeling powerless to get up and answer it. I prayed that I could navigate the three feet between me and it before it stopped ringing. When I did finally pick up, I could barely speak. I must have managed to tell Nan that I needed to go the emergency room because somehow we got there, and somehow my sisters Resa and Judy got there, and I remember sitting in a bed, propped up by pillows, calmly taking a nebulizer treatment while my sisters looked on with tears in their eyes as they remembered seeing my mother years earlier in the same emergency room in a similar bed inhaling a similar nebulizer.

My "neb" was followed by a botched CT scan of my lungs, which was followed by a successful PET scan. No tumors. No pneumonia. My recovery was astonishing: within an hour, I was feeling like a normal person with a bad cold. I was given a bronchodilator (in the form of an inhaler) to take each day and instructed to see my doctor within a week. Nan brought me home, Judy brought me a hamburger, Resa brought me the groceries I needed, and I went to sleep. It goes without saying that my then doctor was out of town, so a week later, I visited a doctor who did not know me. I was officially diagnosed with COPD, given a prescription to refill my bronchodilator, and told to quit smoking immediately. No counseling program, no nicotine patch, no empathy. I did not want to prolong the appointment, so I told the doctor I would try, but even after the previous week's trauma, I still could not imagine quitting. It seems abhorrent to take bronchodilators while willfully negating their effects by smoking, but that is what I did. Even though the shame was eating me alive, my habit continued to will out.

Second. Four months before my exacerbation, I had decided to move from the house that Tom and I had shared for sixteen years and in which I had lived alone for nine years after he died. Here is how it happened. One Sunday morning in March, I was idly paging through the *St. Paul Pioneer Press* when I came across a flyer headlined, "Downtown Loft Living on the Mississippi River." It advertised a condominium building that was so new it was not yet under construction. My mind ignited. I wanted this! A loft is where a person—an artist—like me should live!

I called my friend Sherry, and together we went to the building's sales office, which was a riverside trailer directly across the river from Harriet Island, home of a popular city park featuring a historic pavilion designed by Cap Wigington, the first African American municipal architect in the country, who served for thirty-four years as chief architect for the city of St. Paul. Inside, we encountered a madhouse, a feeding frenzy of potential condo buyers clawing and ripping to acquire the condo of their choice from a selection of floor plans taped to the trailer's walls. Luckily, I acted quickly. It took me just a few minutes to choose my dream condo: a corner one-bedroom-plus-den on the highest floor. As I pondered the floor plan, imagining the placement of my furniture, I was unaware that there was a gathering crowd of condo-hungry Twin Citians behind me, all looking at MY floorplan. Finally, Sherry hissed in my ear, "Do it NOW!" We hailed the salesperson, Sherry wrote a check (because I had not thought to bring my checkbook), and in the nick of time, the deal was done.

Technically, my loft was not a loft. In what I consider a contradiction in terms, the developer called it a "one-level loft" because it had certain features associated with lofts, including high ceilings, huge windows, and exposed heating pipes. No matter the technicality; it was still my dream home. But here, finally, is the point. On that Sunday, I made a pledge that I would never smoke inside my new condo or on the condo's outdoor deck. That meant that I would have to quit smoking before the fall of 2007, when the condo was scheduled to be completed. It is both a grand irony and a perfect example of human nature that in the end, my new condominium would be my reason for quitting, not one of my growing number of morbid medical problems.

Third. A month or two after my exacerbation, I read about a new type of smoking cessation drug that had just come to market. Lauded as a breakthrough, Chantix claimed to work by activating the brain's nicotine receptors so that you are tricked into thinking you have actually ingested nicotine, thus reducing cravings so that your urge to smoke is less intense and therefore easier to resist. The drug had met with success when used to treat gambling addiction, and clinical trials on smokers had proved effective. The protocol sounded humane: you take a low dose of the drug for one week as you continue to smoke, and graduate to a higher dose beginning the day you quit smoking. You then continue for eleven more weeks. If, at the end of that time, you fall off the wagon, you may take a second twelve-week course.

In January 2007, I saw my doctor, got a prescription, and by the following week, I had quit smoking. This simple, straightforward description exactly matches the way it happened, but alas, nothing that hard ends up being that easy. The most common side effect of Chantix is nausea, and for me, it was a redux of an old story. For several days, I vomited during or after every meal. Finally, my brother-in-law Allen called a physician friend who had been a lead researcher in a Minneapolis-based Chantix clinical trial. When he heard that I weighed only 102 pounds, he immediately suggested that I cut my dose in half. The recommended dose, he told Allen, was meant for a much heavier person (a man, I assume), and he assured us that the lower dose would not lessen the drug's effectiveness.

To my relief, the lower dose caused no side effects, and as the weeks went on, I marveled at the way Chantix worked. For the first time in my life, I became wholly cognizant, not merely intellectually informed, of the causal relationship between brain and mind. Not only did I not have the urge to smoke, I no longer even thought about smoking, a spectacular change. The mind of a smoker operates like this: after smoking a cigarette, you feel satisfied, you feel able to clear-mindedly situate yourself in the present moment. For me, that state of being usually lasted for about half an hour. Then my mind would begin to wander. Within a few more minutes, that indistinct absent-mindedness would have grown into a full-on craving for a cigarette. But with Chantix, those cravings disappeared. It dumbfounded me that a drug—a chemical—could have such a precisely targeted effect on consciousness that it could stop someone from craving a cigarette. Apart from my nicotine addiction, which I steadfastly tried to ignore, I had never consciously experienced mind control, and it felt slightly peculiar, almost cultish, as though I were being reeducated. And of course, I was.

I finished my twelve-week Chantix course feeling optimistic. At long last, I was a nonsmoker! But after about fourteen weeks, I began craving cigarettes again (which I later learned was not unusual). Having been smoke-free for so many weeks, one would think that my desire to remain so would be stronger than my desire to smoke, but rather than sanely resisting these urges for the sake of self-preservation, I started cheating. I invented a new series of rationalizations, and to support them, several new ways of behaving. "One can't hurt" was my slogan, but eventually the obvious became apparent to me: if one repeats "One can't hurt" enough times, one ends up with a habit. I can no longer remember how many times I bought an entire pack of cigarettes, smoked one, and after crushing the pack to render the remaining cigarettes unsmokable, deposited it in the trash barrel next to our garage. That was my insurance against temptation. I kept up this pitiful routine for several weeks until even I could not abide such an expensive folly, and then I started a second course of Chantix.

By July 2007, I knew that I would never smoke again. How I knew, I am not sure, but I knew. My chronic bronchitis gradually disappeared. I no longer stunk of smoke. My sense of smell returned. Often during my years of inconsolable sorrow, I had wondered whether the power that my smoking addiction had over me was bolstered by my apathy toward life, because by the time I quit smoking, I was not only addicted to cigarettes, I was also addicted to grief. To the extent that I had been using my smoking habit as a way to prop up my grief, I now began to feel that grip loosen. Most significantly,

I felt liberated. Like an alcoholic, a smoker's life is fashioned around her habit; she literally lives from cigarette to cigarette.

Imagine a Minnesota January, and imagine a woman with emphysema shivering under the eaves of Coffey Hall, the building in which she works. Imagine her chest constricting as she inhales the smoke from her cigarette in the ten-degree air, and imagine her coughing to catch her breath so that she could take the next puff. Then imagine the same scene an hour later, and an hour after that, and an hour after that. Imagine, as she fidgets through two or three or four meetings a day, her attention repeatedly wandering to the next cigarette. Imagine her finger tapping the table, then imagine her shame as she zips her parka. No wonder she can hardly wait to get home to her smokehouse at the end of the day. That is the smoker's prison. To liberate oneself from it is to be reborn. Such liberation is contagious too. Knowing, now, that we have it within us to break a seemingly unending cycle of affliction, shame, and humiliation, we feel freer to confront other ghouls, including prolonged grief, that have been smothering our desire to live.

4

Leave Your Grief at Home
and Do Your Work at the Office

A YEAR AFTER TOM'S DEATH, I was more dead than alive. I no longer listened to music. I no longer had an easel. My paints were gathering dust in the attic. All my life, I had lived for art. (This is factually true. I made my first mural at the age of one, on the wall above my crib, by finger-painting excrement that had fallen out of my diaper.) I had spent my entire life creating things, whether drawn, painted, sculpted, knitted, written, composed, or dramatized. (I had a brief childhood career as an actress at St. Paul's Edyth Bush Theater, where I made a name playing Drizella, one of Cinderella's ugly sisters.) The only occupation that could turn me away from art was reading, which I did for long stretches while sitting in the midst of the chaos that was our too-small-for-six-kids home. That was how I learned to shut out the mayhem whirling around me and focus without interruption on the realm contained in whatever book I was reading. All my life, I had been a busy bee: occupied, engaged, absorbed. But now I was no longer that self.

From my first day of widowhood, I felt suddenly and strangely unlike myself. I remember the feeling vividly because it was tactile: it made my skin crawl. I felt exposed, I felt naked, I felt awkward, I felt deformed. I felt paranoid. I was no longer one more unrecognizable being in a large, lonely crowd. Now I was the sore thumb, the oddity, the one at whom you stare as a child and from whom you avert your gaze as an adult. Physically, I knew I was intact, but I felt like an amputee. It was not that I imagined that people, whether family members or strangers on the street, could somehow see into me and gawk at my grief. It was that without Tom at my side, I no longer felt whole; I no longer felt at ease in the world. I no longer fit, and that profoundly embarrassed me.

I began dreading my forays into the everyday humdrum of St. Paul, Minnesota, because I was afraid that I would accidentally encounter someone I knew, especially a distant acquaintance who might not know what had happened to Tom, to me. I certainly had acquired enough acquaintances over the years, especially in my professional life. What would I say? How could I open my mouth without crying? How could I pretend, even in passing, that all was well, when in truth, I could hardly keep my knees from giving out from under me? I had never trusted blithely, but now I trusted no one. No wonder I decided that my best defense against being misunderstood or humiliated was to hole up at home and venture out only as needed for work, medical appointments, and necessary errands.

Like a self-fulfilling prophecy, these feelings, which I now understand were extreme if not downright abnormal, were reinforced anytime I happened to chance upon an acquaintance during an outing. Once, during that first September, on an errand to Pier 1 to shop for some long-forgotten necessity, I encountered Cheryl, who had worked for a while as a member of our Duluth-based Split Rock Arts Program summer staff. She was perfectly suited to her people-centered job because she was outgoing, confident, caring, and resourceful. But in Pier 1 that day, those qualities, which I had valued so much in our work environment, transduced when I told her about Tom, rendering her inappropriately loud, embarrassingly dramatic, and physically overbearing, all in the space of two or three minutes. First, she began crying noisily when I told her my news, even though she had hardly known Tom, and then she embraced me in a bear hug that nearly crushed me to death. How I extricated myself from the situation I do not recall, but I assume it was quickly and I know it was resolutely.

That first November, my family had convinced me that it was important for me to attend Thanksgiving dinner, before which Tom would not be making the mashed potatoes he had made each Thanksgiving for the past twenty years. They must have felt that I would have been more miserable at home alone, eating (or not) a prepackaged frozen entrée. Our family gathering, held at my aunt and uncle's condominium, was an evening affair rather than a midday feast, and arrival time may have been around five o'clock. My memories of that morning and afternoon, while not minute-to-minute specific, are nonetheless vivid: the day was interminable. As I waited hour after hour for five o'clock to arrive, I gradually worked myself into a frenzy of anxiety. How could I bear to face my relatives? How would I manage to get through the evening? Would I be able to eat without vomiting? And what would I say when my family started asking why I was not eating? What if I started crying for no reason? What if someone asked about Tom? What if someone asked how I was doing? What would I say? That I wished I were dead?

As the afternoon wore on, my dread of going out into the cold and dark intensified, and I contemplated calling my sister Nan, telling her that I would not be going to dinner, and asking her to make my excuses. Once that deed was done, I could undress, don my flannel nightgown and quilted cotton robe, and relax with the evening football game. But something—call it my inner parent—stopped me from doing that. The parent reproached me for my grief: I had to resume normal activities sometime, and I had to stop babying myself. After all, it had been four whole months since Tom died. Buck up, it scolded. I went to Thanksgiving dinner. I recall nothing of the evening except that I ducked out immediately after dessert, which I did not eat.

As I was driving home, I made a promise to myself. I would never again be pressured into doing anything that triggered such acute emotional discomfort within me, even if loved and respected others were attempting to convince me that the anything under consideration was for my own good. How can something that throws you into emotional turmoil, even for a day, be good for you? No one knows me better than me, I concluded, even though my capacity for self-insight had died with Tom four months earlier. Once having made my resolution, it was astonishingly easy to skip family gatherings without feeling guilty, and decline professional and social invitations that I knew I would dread having to attend when the appointed date arrived.

My extended family, consisting of my mother's brother and sister-in-law and their children, all of whom I loved, and my immediate family, consisting then of my parents, my five siblings and three siblings-in-law, and their children, all of whom I loved, gathered for four grand holiday celebrations each year: Rosh Hashanah (Jewish New Year), Thanksgiving, Hanukkah, and Passover, when we held a traditional seder. Tom and I looked forward to all of them, but especially to Passover, when my mother, my three sisters, and I would spend three days cooking and otherwise preparing for our large seder, which also included a small assortment of friends that might change from year to year.

Then Tom died. In an instant, or perhaps a week or a few weeks, the spiritual lift that family holiday celebrations had afforded me since childhood vanished. No one will miss me, I told myself. After all, I was only one member of a large, talkative family, and my presence or absence mattered little to the overall merriment of the event. The world, whether my family, my friends, or my professional community, will hardly notice. The paradox of feeling naked to the world was feeling invisible in it. How I was perceived by others, I do not know, and I did not bother to consider. I did not care. I no longer remember how long it took me to feel comfortable enough to resume attending family gatherings, but I imagine it must have been at least three or four years.

*

On Wednesday, September 1, 1999, just over thirteen months after Tom's death, another death occurred, this time at my workplace. Our unit, then called Continuing Education and Extension (CEE), was one of the largest university continuing education units in the country because the University of Minnesota's Twin Cities campus was located smack in the middle of a metropolitan area of three million people. CEE offered community members access to their flagship university through evening and correspondence courses that allowed one to earn a degree, obtain continuing education in one's profession, and partake in over two hundred not-for-credit lifelong learning courses in the liberal arts. For decades, CEE used revenue generated from its evening courses to fund programs that it felt were important, but unlike credit-bearing academic programs, could not produce enough revenue to cover their costs. That was how my department, Continuing Education in the Arts, was able to exist.

But in 1998, CEE's bubble burst. The University's central administration finally decided to scrutinize CEE's budget closely enough to discover that the unit was sitting on a gluttonous pile of cash and carrying reserves that would have been appropriate for a much larger unit. Our longtime dean resigned (which may or may not have been a coincidence), CEE's budget was restructured to include long-overdue revenue sharing with the academic colleges that provided CEE's instructors and courses, an interim dean was installed, and an organizational development expert from the University's business school (who was later hired to serve as our permanent dean) was enlisted to create a strategic plan for CEE.

A brilliant and beloved Minnesota writer, the late Paul Gruchow, once told me that "the University uses a heck of a lot of energy just to stand still." Truer words were never spoken. Over the ensuing year, CEE was reorganized, subsuming its smaller, freestanding departments into larger, less costly umbrella units. And oh yes, our name had to be changed in order to stop, once and for all, any confusion with the University of Minnesota Extension Service, which served the state's vast rural areas through its land grant mission. We went from

Continuing Education and Extension to the College of Continuing Education. Now, at last, we were a college rather than a (lowly) service. Acronymically, we went from CEE to CCE. Names of entities within large universities are important insofar as they must be indicative, but if you think of a name as, for example, a suit of clothes, it is the body within the suit that ultimately matters more, and therein lay the rub.

To help the staff prepare for the unit's organizational changes, our interim dean, who, in an interesting noncoincidence, had also served a stint as interim dean of the Minnesota Extension Service, contracted with a "transformation" consultant, a genial St. Paulite with a master's degree in educational psychology and a spectacularly coiffed head of perfect ringlets. On the aforementioned September 1, 1999, an all-staff program was held to introduce the unit's new name and give us a chance to interact in small groups with colleagues with whom we would shortly be sharing a work space.

The program's theme was something along the lines of "out with the old, in with the new," and its goal was to encourage us to let go of outdated structures and processes. One can imagine that an engaging expression of this theme might have been a workplace-appropriate, off-season New Year's celebration, perhaps featuring a diapered baby doll, to symbolize our fresh new name and structure, but that was not what happened. To carry out their theme, the interim dean and transformation consultant brought in an actual coffin and a recording of a choir singing funereal music. Each small group was instructed to select a representative to share highlights of its conversation with the full group, and was made to stand in front of the coffin while doing so. Rather than merely leaving old ways behind, it looked as though the new CCE wanted to kill them.

The sight of an actual coffin undid me. I was shocked. I wanted to flee and thought hard for a few seconds about doing so. My tears rose up, but I managed to stifle them. With a hundred people assembled in what was supposed to be a professional setting, I only wanted to compose myself so I could begin contemplating what I would say to the transformation consultant about this freakish affront. (I had temporarily forgotten that I needed my job.) I asked Carol Daly whether she thought the coffin stunt was tasteless, and she said it was insensitive. I thought it was both, and I also thought it was offensive, disgusting, perverse, perverted, bizarre, stupid, juvenile, inappropriate, macabre, thoughtless, irresponsible, and here feel free to add your own adjectives.

After the interminable program ended, I approached the transformation consultant and genially told her that I thought using an actual coffin as a symbol of progress was insensitive. I looked her in the eye and earnestly explained that Carol and I had both lost our husbands recently, and we both reacted negatively to the presence of a coffin at a professional program. I reassured her that I was mentioning this so that she would not make the same mistake twice, since one never knows who among an assembled group might be bereaved. She told me that they had thought long and hard about the coffin and understood that it was "a little unusual," but that they were "really trying to put some fun into the meeting."

*

This incident heralded the beginning of the end of my University career. Seen in the light of time, it was emblematic of the ways in which my work environment was evolving. The millennial fin de siècle was a time of government belt-tightening in Minnesota, and as the University's public funding dwindled, central administrators saw fit to reduce CCE's funding in similar measure. As the University's academic priorities evolved toward science and technology and away from liberal and fine arts, so too did CCE's programming priorities. Our newly formed department, Personal Enrichment Programs, housed CCE's most vulnerable arts and humanities programs, including the Split Rock Arts Program. These programs existed on the margins of the University's mission because most of them did not carry academic credits (the currency of the University), most could not earn enough revenue to cover their expenses, and most did not offer continuing education in one's profession. No matter that the arts and humanities are essential to human civilization, and without them, our species could not survive.

In addition to its myriad other benefits, Split Rock was the country's most exhilarating, memorable way to earn two graduate-level academic credits in only a week. We had thousands of effusive evaluations from participants and instructors to prove this, and we had a veritable army of past participants, some of whom were donors to the University, who were ready to enthusiastically defend the program. All of us on the staff had heard the sweet music of praise from participants: "It changed my life!" "It went way beyond anything I could have imagined!" "It was the most memorable experience of my life!" Had the University tried to eliminate Split Rock, we wanted to make sure there would be an outcry heard throughout Minnesota and beyond.

During my first two decades at the University, I had been fortunate to work under two successive supervisors who gave me the freedom to direct Split Rock in my own way. They trusted me and appreciated my work. They treated me as an equal, a partner, and a colleague. They were also busy with their own work, so they were grateful that I preferred to work independently. Both had offices that were distant from mine, and they did not, and did not want to, keep track of my daily comings and goings.

But now things would change. An accomplished arts leader who had had a long career at a major local arts center had been hired to lead Personal Enrichment Programs. I will call her Austen. As a senior member of this brand-new department, I would now be working under a full-time supervisor whose office was next to mine. I had been acquainted with Austen before she came to the University and had always liked her. But now our relationship would change. As we spent more time working together, our differences began to show. Had I not already been feeling sick and tired of my job, I might not have felt them as much, but I was still suffering from deadening grief, and that shaded every aspect of my life, including my behavior at work. All things considered, what I most needed at the time was the longest leash possible, and that was not Austen's style.

First, there was my smoking problem. It did not nettle me as much when I was interacting with others, whether in meetings, informal conversations, or on the telephone, but when I had to buckle down at my desk and tackle complicated writing projects or financial tasks, I simply could not concentrate long enough to accomplish anything. I needed a cigarette more often than I could leave the building to have one. I longed to smoke in my own basement whenever I wanted, and I wanted frequently. Between my grief and my nicotine addiction, I lived in a double-walled prison of my own making.

Second, there was my computer problem. In the late 1980s, each CEE staff member was assigned an Apple Macintosh computer. Not long after that, Tom and I bought a Mac, along with an incomparable Apple Laserwriter printer, using his employer's interest-free computer loan program. This meant that my computer capabilities at home were actually better than those at work because I had a printer at my desk rather than in a utility room down the hall. Then, sometime in the middle 1990s, CEE replaced our Macs with less expensive Dell personal computers. It was a precipitous fall from grace. In a day, I went from using a highly intuitive, impeccably designed tool to a revoltingly inelegant, cheap clunker. Worst, I was now incompatible. Any document I created at home on my Mac formatted itself differently on my PC and vice versa. Even Microsoft Word and Excel behaved differently on the PC than they did on the Mac, which meant that I was constantly wasting time reformatting my documents. Discomfort makes one taut, and this particular discomfort drove me crazy.

I lived with this problem by creating and printing all my important documents at home. I used my PC at work only for on-screen reading and email correspondence. To maintain this cockamamie practice, I worked for about three hours at home early each morning and then put in a full day at my office. Every evening since Tom's death, I had been going to bed immediately after dinner so I could watch television under the covers. I would take my sleep medication (trazodone, an antidepressant, which I still take today), at about eight o'clock and was asleep by eight thirty. I awoke between three thirty and four thirty, and after a first cup of coffee, a first bite of toast, and a first cigarette, I booted up the computer and started working. I stopped working at seven thirty in order to give myself time to shower, dress, drive to campus, and arrive at my office no later than about nine o'clock. Austen always arrived at about nine thirty, and I felt that I would be above reproach as long as my arrival preceded hers.

This mini-hell went on for five years. Early on, I had asked Austen if I could arrange to work at home one day each week, and she had refused. I cannot remember whether she felt it would set a bad example for the staff, whether she felt my presence in the office was needed every damned day come hell or high water, or whether she felt she might be violating some rule or another by granting my request. Thankfully, it no longer matters. I do remember that I was not surprised by her decision because I already knew that her reason was that she could not keep watch over me if I were not in the office. The awful truth was that she did not trust me or any other members of her staff. By her own admission, she felt that when the cat was away, the mice would play, and we were her mice.

Because the University offered a generous benefit package, and because I was a longtime employee, I had banked about four months of vacation leave. Having no one to go with, I had nowhere to go, so I began using vacation time to work at home, a new low for me (and anyone). One might think that nearly unlimited vacation leave would be worth its weight in gold, especially if you plan to travel the entire Alaska Highway, as Tom and I had hoped to do, but in truth, it is a self-limiting perquisite. To do one's job, one must put in the time. That is why I had vacation earnings to spare.

Third and finally, there was my I-hate-work-and-desperately-want-to-retire problem. This was the deeper hell. Some who are grieving find not only distraction but solace and even healing in their work, but for me, dragging myself to the office each day; cultivating and continuing the human relationships required for my job, including and most important, those with my staff; and executing a steady stream of complicated management and programmatic tasks felt like climbing Mount Everest. By the time I got home at day's end, I felt as though I had, indeed, climbed and descended that giant mountain. It was no wonder I was in bed by six thirty in the evening.

I was trapped. Though I would have felt trapped by my smoking problem alone, and I would have felt trapped by my computer problem alone, having an uncomfortable relationship with my supervisor meant that I never felt truly at ease in my workplace. That alone would have been enough to make me hate going to work, or so I thought. Now, as I write and because I write, my vision has cleared, and time has miniaturized these seemingly insoluble predicaments. The truth is that had these troubles not been bound in a straitjacket of overriding, unabating grief, I believe that I might have been able to more easily resolve each of them. But because it impairs one's judgment, grief narrows the mind. One loses the ability to take in stride the everyday challenges that life presents, and because my intense grief lasted so long, I habitually acted against my own interests, as well as those of the people I loved.

5

Complicated Grief

THE TEENAGE SON of Carol Daly's sister was murdered several years before Carol and I lost our husbands. After the tragedy, Carol's sister joined a professionally facilitated support group for parents of murdered children, where she learned that acute grieving can last as long as ten years after one's child is murdered. The same is true if one's child or longtime life partner commits suicide. The point is obvious: the visible shape of grief and the time given over to it can vary depending on the nature of the loss. It can also vary depending on how attracted we are to our grief, how dependent we are on it, and how necessary it is to our survival. I was attracted, dependent, and needy, and after a year or two or three, I began adjusting to living in grief. My sadness had become a protective cocoon, freeing me from responsibility, ambition, and the intrinsic uncertainty of hope.

That is why at eight o'clock on the evening of Tuesday, October 29, 2002, I was doing what I had done every night for the past four years: reclining in bed, my head propped against the pillows, watching television. But on this night, rather than being lulled into drowsiness by *Nature* or *Nova*, I was sobbing uncontrollably as I watched, crying harder and longer and more gut-wrenchingly than I had since the first months after Tom's death. Like a baby left alone in the pitch-dark, I was bawling with so much force that I was making myself sick to my stomach in addition to being sick at heart. Along with thousands of my fellow Minnesotans, I was watching one of the most heartbreaking events of my life, a live telecast of a memorial service for someone whom millions of Americans, including me, had loved and lost in an unthinkable tragedy: Senator Paul Wellstone, dead at age fifty-eight.

Four days earlier, on October 25, our beloved senator, along with his wife, Sheila Wellstone, his daughter, Marcia Wellstone, and five others were killed in a plane crash two miles south of Eveleth, Minnesota, a mining town about sixty miles north of Duluth in the heart of the Mesabi Iron Range. Low clouds had blanketed the area that morning. The pilot and copilot were flying on instrument flight rules, but instead of guiding them to the airport, the route prescribed by their instruments repeatedly circled them back to the heavily forested crash site. Still, the National Transportation Safety Board, along with friends and colleagues of the pilot, speculated that the crash may have been at least partially the result of pilot error.

Senator Wellstone and his party were bound for Eveleth to attend the funeral of the father of a friend. To do so, the senator had passed up a chance to attend a fundraiser in Minneapolis at which Democratic powerhouses Walter Mondale and Ted Kennedy were scheduled to speak. The crash happened just eleven days before he would have almost certainly been elected to serve a third term. Politically, much hung in the balance. Senator Wellstone's reelection was critical to the Democratic Party retaining its majority in the United States Senate, and control of the Senate was critical to Democrats because the presidency and the House of Representatives were in Republican hands. In the 2002 election, Republican Norm Coleman (a former Democrat, or, as my father called him, "a turncoat") was elected to represent Minnesota, narrowly defeating former vice president Walter Mondale, who had volunteered to replace Wellstone on the ballot. Indeed, it was this election that allowed Republicans to gain a majority in the Senate in 2003. (In 2008, Al Franken defeated Coleman in his bid for reelection.)

But on that October night in 2002, I was not mourning for the Democratic Party's likely loss of a senate seat. It never crossed my mind. I, along with the rest of the country, was grieving the loss of a selfless human being whose every thought was for the welfare of his fellow humans, who cared nothing for power for its own sake, who spoke true words of justice and always acted in accordance with them, who steadfastly resisted corruption, bigotry, and violence, and who, as "the moral conscience of the Senate," understood that compromise is an ethical art. Paul Wellstone was a giant among us.

The nationally broadcast memorial service was held at Williams Arena on the University of Minnesota campus in Minneapolis. In attendance were political dignitaries of every stripe, including former president Bill Clinton, half the members of the U.S. Senate, and thousands of broken-hearted citizens who had come to mourn with Wellstone's two living sons, his extended family, and his loving friends. It seemed to take forever for the visiting politicians to arrive and get settled, and during that time, a popular Twin Cities musical group, Sounds of Blackness, sang "Love Train" over and over and over again. *People all over the world, join hands / start a love train, love train.* An appealing melody, a catchy rhythm, and the group members' beautiful voices made an ideal anthem for a celebration of Wellstone's life.

I had studiously avoided listening to music for over four years, and now, hearing this mesmerizing chorus over and over and over again, I felt ambushed by it. The music alone would have been enough to plunge me into a hole of grief even deeper than the one in which I was already trapped, but as I watched the memorial service, I could feel in my shuddering body that listening to "Love Train" seemed to intensify the agonizing sense of loss I had felt since the day of the crash. No wonder I was crying my heart out. No wonder I was sick to my stomach. No wonder I was surrendering to a musical ambush. I had just experienced the most significant loss of a loved one since I lost Tom.

Yes. Of course we can love a person whom we have never met. We may not have physical proximity to our beloved, but knowing that he or she is in the world enhances us and the world. Our beloved makes us happy simply by virtue of being the person he or she is and doing what he or she does in the world. This way of loving makes us more loving, and that makes the world better. Losing someone that we, along with like-minded others, have loved from a distance can affect us as profoundly as losing someone we knew and loved in our daily lives.

The Chilean poet Pablo Neruda put it this way in "Childhood and Poetry":

To feel the love of people whom we love is a fire that feeds our life. But to feel the affection that comes from those whom we do not know, from those unknown to us, who are watching over our sleep and solitude, over our dangers and our weaknesses—that is something still greater and more beautiful because it widens out the boundaries of our being, and unites all living things.

Two years after Paul Wellstone's death, when my mother died, and again five years after that when my father died, I came to understand that once you have experienced a life-shattering loss, every loss you suffer thereafter revives the grief you felt from your previous losses. Imagine a thinly scabbed wound that reopens again and again with the slightest stress: the result is that the wound never completely heals and so remains permanently vulnerable to reinjury. Each time you hear, see, or read about someone else's significant loss, you grieve again, especially when that loss feels similar to yours. This is not recurring self-pity but an expanded capacity for empathy, a broader opening of the heart that I could not have felt had I not lost Tom.

*

Persistently, as I write, I think of the German philosopher Walter Benjamin's angel of history, which he described after viewing Paul Klee's painting *Angelus Novus*:

> This is how one pictures the angel of history. His face is turned toward the past. Where we perceive a chain of events, he sees one single catastrophe which keeps piling wreckage upon wreckage and hurls it in front of his feet. The angel would like to stay, awaken the dead, and make whole what has been smashed. But a storm is blowing from Paradise; it

has got caught in his wings with such violence that the angel can no longer close them. This storm irresistibly propels him into the future to which his back is turned while the pile of debris before him grows skyward.

Even though our losses continue to accumulate as our lives grow longer, we expect our coping skills to keep pace. We are expected to recover from even our most grievous losses by traveling a relatively straightforward psychological progression from bereavement (the actual loss) to grief (our responses to that loss) to mourning (learning to live with our loss) to recovery (restoration of a satisfying, meaningful life). Along this path we might encounter ditches and detours, but experts say that our bodies and minds are built for resilience, and that recovery from acute or "active" grief is as normal as grief itself. But what if we cannot meet those expectations? What if this so-called recovery is somehow disrupted or undermined? What if these "normal" processes take an abnormally long time to take hold? What if they fail us altogether? What if something inside us will not allow us to release ourselves and move forward?

Western psychiatry and related professions have created an assortment of names for grief that is too intense and lasts too long, including "unresolved grief," "prolonged grief disorder," and "persistent complex bereavement disorder." The most common is "complicated grief," a medical term for a "superimposed process that alters grief and modifies its course for the worse." Grief is considered complicated if it continues to be acute at least a year after the loss **and** if the bereaved person is experiencing persistent yearning or longing for the person who has died, a recurring desire to die in order to be reunited with that person, refusal to believe that the grieving person's loved one is really gone forever, inappropriately intense reactions to memories of the person who has died, and "distress or impairment in social, occupational, or other important areas of functioning."

Though I have selected these criteria from a list of a dozen proffered in a journal article by Dr. M. Katherine Shear, founder and director of Columbia University's Center for Complicated Grief, I did not cherry-pick them to sweeten my story. To my shock, almost all of them perfectly described what I had felt for far too long. Now I can see that my reaction to Paul Wellstone's death was not only genuine heartbreak but also an expression of complicated grief. In characterizing this syndrome, Shear says that ultimately the normal grieving process "leads to acceptance of the inevitability of the loss, integration of its reality into ongoing life, and reimagining a future with the possibility of joy and satisfaction. During this journey, acute grief, intensely painful and dominant, becomes integrated, muted, and in the background. CG [complicated grief] is the syndrome that occurs when this transformation does not occur." Only now, more than two decades on, do I finally understand that what I was experiencing was not normal, that it was a medically acknowledged "disorder," and that perhaps I could have sought professional help to treat it.

But during the years I lived inside my concrete-block grief cell, my capacity for level-headed self-evaluation had so diminished that it never occurred to me to take action on behalf of my own emotional health. Within the thick confines of such a tiny existence, one becomes entirely fatalistic: a crushed, dispirited prisoner is not able to resist her jailer, especially when that jailer is a force beyond human reach, a force some would call God and some would call Fate. I never questioned that my only choice was to wait it out. I could not have consciously taken a step back to consider whether my sadness had metastasized into a disease. Without consideration, I had accepted the fact that my ways of grieving merely exaggerated traits that I had always known in myself: introversion, obsession, guilt, self-criticism.

Now I could add another: self-absorption. After Tom died, I no longer had my partner in life, the one whose well-being meant more to me than my own, the one whom I cared for in sickness, the first recipient of whatever spiritual generosity I possessed, the one whose happiness ensured mine, the one to whom I gave my deepest love. Over time, my grief had become my life, and it came before everyone and everything else. If Tom and I had had children, perhaps my decline into self-centeredness could have been prevented or at least kept at bay, but we were childless by choice, and this was a consequence. I felt myself emotionally disabled, and I acted the part without regard to its effects on those I loved, its sabotage of my work, and the ways in which it undermined my physical health.

Experts tell us that yearning for the deceased, missing the deceased, emotional pain and numbness, and loneliness are the four most common "affective experiences" associated with complicated grief. In fact, these particular sufferings hallmark the disorder. Specifically, writes Mary-Frances O'Connor, a psychologist at the University of Arizona who studies emotions experienced by people suffering from complicated grief, "persistent intense yearning for the deceased is a core clinical feature of complicated grief (CG) that distinguishes it from other mental disorders that develop following loss." By "other mental disorders," she means primarily depression (which may or may not affect people who suffer from complicated grief) and post-traumatic stress disorder.

For at least seven years, I yearned for Tom without abatement, and I missed him passionately and constantly. Though I could have never parsed these emotions so closely then, I have now come to learn that there is not only a clinical difference between yearning for someone and missing someone; there is also a defining difference by which complicated grief earns its name. Yearning, according to O'Connor and her coauthors, is "an unsatisfied, intense, and future-oriented appetitive desire. It is not merely missing something from the past (i.e. being aware of its absence), but rather entails actively desiring something in the future." The implication is that as time goes on, and the presence of the one we miss recedes farther into the past, we will probably not miss him as much. But when we yearn, we are desiring both a present and a future with our lost beloved. As long as we continue to yearn, the passage of time is irrelevant. There is no mediating influence to ease our longing. It is, by its nature, insatiable because the object of our desire is dead.

In the early months and extending on for perhaps two years, I heard Tom at night in our small home, walking to the bathroom, opening or closing the refrigerator, rustling the sheets as he got into or out of bed, opening the back door so he could have a midnight smoke on our back steps. Sometimes a dream would follow his noises; other times I would lie alert in bed, waiting for him to come back. I heard him in the daytime, too, loading his work clothes into the washing machine, plopping an ice cube into his milk, creaking his chair as he ruffled through the newspaper on the front porch. After a long while, I no longer associated the ordinary sounds emanating from an aging house with him. Instead, my yearning settled into a self-contained ache, acute in its intensity but chronic in its duration. Like an inflamed sciatic nerve, it often hurt to the edge of insanity.

In 2008, O'Connor, then part of a research group at the University of California, Los Angeles, studied a small group of women who had lost a mother or sister to breast cancer. About half of them had recovered from their grief normally, but the other half were suffering from complicated grief. While undergoing an MRI brain scan, each of the study's subjects was shown photographs of her deceased loved one followed by photographs of strangers. The results suggested that "long-term or 'complicated' grief activates neurons in the reward centers of the brain, possibly giving these memories addiction-like properties." Importantly, this response did not occur in the brains of subjects whose grief had taken a normal course.

O'Connor cautioned that "she is not suggesting that such reveries about the deceased are emotionally satisfying, but rather that they may serve in some people as a type of craving for the reward response that may make adapting to the reality of the loss more difficult." In other words, these study subjects continued to crave the same pleasurable response they used to have upon seeing a picture of their loved one when she was alive, but because that craving was impossible to satisfy, it conspired to prevent them from reconciling themselves to their loss.

Call it craving. Call it yearning. No matter what you call it, the massive heartache that kept me steeped in misery year after year also kept me fiercely, if insidiously, connected to Tom. As the UCLA study suggests, could it have been the craving itself that kept me grieving? What would have happened if I had somehow been able to quiet that longing? Would it have meant that Tom and I were no longer bonded? Would it have meant that I no longer loved him? I wonder now if that insatiable yearning was a perverted way of proving to myself that I still loved him. It is possible. I had lived so close to my grief for so long that it had become a suffocating sedative. Gradually, my inability to imagine life without Tom had become an inability to imagine life without grief.

There was my insistent yearning, and there was also my desire to die in order to be with Tom, which for nearly four years kept me from feeling a preference for life. Though I would now characterize my death wish as half-hearted, I felt it strongly enough at the time so that it killed my desire to survive. A will to live, a self-preservation instinct: both had disappeared. Before Tom died, Carol Daly told me to save his drugs. "Don't let hospice take them back," she advised. "You never know." I bagged up his liquid morphine, oxycontin, and codeine. There was also Ativan, but I appropriated that for my own use so that I could sleep at night. I counted the oxycontin and codeine tablets, and reckoned that there were more than enough to do the job without resorting to the almost-full bottle of morphine. I kept the bag in our linen closet, and every time I opened the door to grab a towel or put away the freshly laundered bedsheets, I gazed at the bag. But somehow the moment was never quite right. After all my consideration and contemplation, not once did I come close to suicide by overdose. I was simply too afraid. Gradually, my preference for death was replaced by apathy. If I lived, I lived. If I died, I died.

It seems like an unbelievable paradox even to me, but at the same time as I endured constant, unbearable yearning for

Tom and a deeply serious, if ambivalent, wish to join him in death, I could not bear to remember him. I now know that this insidious disability was one more expression of complicated grief, the one that Shear characterizes as "inappropriately intense reactions to memories of the person who has died." It was a true dichotomy: at the same time as I yearned for him, I could not bear to bring him to mind. It was simply too painful. The trouble was that, at least in the first few years of widowhood, I was haunted by recollections of his physical decline as his disease worsened and plagued by memories of him as he was when he was mortally ill.

Chemotherapy that his doctors surely knew would never cure him served only to give him false hope. He might wake up one morning in unusually good spirits, having noticed that a softball-sized malignant lymph node in his neck seemed to have shrunk a little after a chemo treatment, only to wake up the following morning to see that another node in his neck, which just the day before had been the size of a walnut, had grown overnight to the size of an egg. Within a few weeks after he started treatment, his thick, wavy hair (except for his runt of a ponytail, which I cut off before it was too late) was gone, as were his eyebrows. His lung capacity was so diminished that he had to pause to catch his breath after walking from the bathroom to the kitchen, and I can still see him leaning over the counter, panting as he whispered, "I just want to do what I used to do." Two weeks before he died, his dental bridge, which had been part of him since he lost a front tooth in a Navy training exercise, fell out. He had lost so much weight that it no longer fit.

These, along with countless similar others, were the memories that day after day, week after week, month after month, and year after year I worked with all my might to shut off the moment they flooded my consciousness. To help drive them from my mind, I tried to force myself to think of Tom as he was when he was well, but even those memories were too painful to bear. I was tormented: not only had my beloved—the object of my yearning—become physically inaccessible to me, but I could not even bear to hold him in my own mind.

How are we affected when there are people and experiences in our pasts that are too painful to remember but too essential to forget? How are we affected when memories of them, including the feelings they evoke, persist for years on end, simmering just below our consciousness and coming up for air when we least expect it? To carry on living, we work hard to stifle these memories, but even as we do so, we know that if, in a selective amnesia, we were able to completely and irretrievably forget what is too painful to remember, we would lose integral parts of ourselves, leaving us irreparably broken for the rest of our lives.

How can the inability to remember one's lost loved one exist alongside the refusal to believe that one's lost loved one is really gone forever? In dreams. While we cannot censor our sleeping dreams, we forget most of them upon waking, which amounts to the same thing. Over the past two decades, I have had dozens of dreams in which Tom either came back from the dead or never died in the first place. Still, in a contradiction to what scientists have observed in people suffering from complicated grief, I am convinced that one reason my grief was so acute and persistent was that I *did* believe he was gone forever. The unreality lay in my inability to accept that fact: *My husband is gone forever. He will never come back. Now my job is to carry on living without him.*

As the years passed, it became obvious that he was gone forever and that I was carrying on without him. Still, I continue to ask: Are our lost loved ones really gone forever? Are they obliterated except in memory? Yesterday I wrote the preceding paragraph, and coincidentally or not, last night as I slept, I dreamed that Tom had never left. Coincidentally or not, when I awoke this morning, I remembered the dream. I was walking with my sister Resa at an outdoor gathering, perhaps the Minnesota State Fair, and without our noticing, afternoon had turned to evening. To be exact, it was 6:15 p.m. It was dark save for the lighted streets. We had stopped to discuss whether to leave the gathering, and as we were talking, I happened to turn my head. There was Tom walking toward us, hale and vigorous, his backpack on his back. As he grew closer, I held out my arms to welcome him, but instead of embracing me, he hung his head, hunched his shoulders, and crumpled to the ground like an exhausted marathon runner who has just crossed the finish line. I came to the ground and sat next to him, resting my head against his bent knee as he told us a story about where he had been. I cannot remember his words.

6

Distress in Occupational Functioning

IT IS NOT SURPRISING that one of the most common indicators of complicated grief is "distress or impairment in social, occupational, or other important areas of functioning." Though I have no doubt that I suffered distress and impairment in nearly every area of psychological functioning, my job, above all else, stood between me and destitution. Destitution is more than a state of mind, it is a desperate state of living that might include homelessness, starvation, and untreated disease. When you are already feeling at sea, aimlessly drifting with no land in sight and halfheartedly holding on to keep from drowning, losing your job could well be the breach that sinks your lifeboat.

By the fall of 2002, my work situation had become so difficult that rightly or wrongly, I feared for my future every day. Then, in a self-fulfilling prophecy, came the breach that sank the boat. In November, the Split Rock Arts Program was evicted from the University's Duluth campus, our summer home since 1984. Late one Friday afternoon, I received a short email message from the chair of the Duluth art department, whom I will call Ardis, saying that Split Rock would no longer be able to use her department's studios for our workshops, and we should plan to relocate in time for the following summer's program. Period.

My husband was dead and now someone was about to kill my child. I cried all weekend, but it was not enough. Thus far, my tears had not brought Tom back to me, and now they would not save Split Rock. I was paralyzed by stress. I could not live for even a weekend with the Rock of Gibraltar on my shoulders. I needed to decide on some kind of next step, an initial salvo in defense of my program, and that meant that I had to find a way forward by searching my own psyche. My intuition had always been my most reliable resource in surviving life's vicissitudes, and now I urgently needed to put it to practical use. I was in a vise. No one in my unit, not Austen, not our dean, not the associate dean who had once been my supervisor, would be able to advocate to higher powers for a way out of this. Each University campus had complete discretion over its own affairs, and I knew that this decision would not be overruled, not even by the president, who loved Split Rock.

Though Ardis had given no reason for her decision, I knew from our long history that it was political in nature and had to do with punishing the supercilious marauders from the hegemonic Twin Cities campus who had been invading her department and colonizing her studios every summer for the past nineteen years. In my stew, I began thinking back on my relationship with her. The more I thought about her, the worse the relationship got, at least in my roiling mind. Yes, she had always been a cold fish, she had always resented Split Rock, and she had always been a person who never explained herself. The fact that she was an interesting, talented artist was beside the point. How was I to reason with her? How could I appeal to her?

After two days and a record-breaking number of cigarettes, I came to a decision. I would schedule a meeting with Ardis as soon as possible. First, I needed to learn why she was expelling us so that I could better assess our options. Second, our planning for the coming summer was well under way. We had already hired most of our workshop teachers, so I would tell her that we needed to use her studios for one more summer. If she tried to deny us that small mercy, especially considering that without Split Rock, those very studios would remain empty all summer, I would inform her that I intended to plead our one-last-summer case at the presidential level. After the meeting, I would begin exploring a fresh start for Split Rock on the University's Twin Cities campus, where the program could reside in its resource-rich academic home, rather than renting facilities at a University campus whose academic life was separate from ours.

First thing Monday morning I shared Ardis's email with Austen, who was genuinely distressed that anyone could send such a cruel email message, especially late on a Friday afternoon. Then I told her my plan. She agreed with my next steps and was anxious to support me in any way she could. On Friday of that week, she and I drove to Duluth to meet with Ardis. The flat gray sky matched our mood, but the weather in Duluth cooperated: there was no fog and no snow. The meeting lasted no more than half an hour. We sat at a rectangular table, Austen and I next to each other and a stone-hearted

Ardis directly across from me. When I asked her why she wanted to evict Split Rock, she said simply, "The faculty doesn't want you here."

That was as much as we would learn, except that she also mentioned that changes were afoot in her department. To survive, the department had decided to focus its curriculum on graphic design. Some of its fine art courses would be eliminated, and several of its art studios would be converted to computer-based design studios. I asked her for one more summer, and she immediately agreed, but there was no hope of further negotiation. One way or another, Split Rock's twenty-year run in Duluth was coming to an end. Austen and I drove home. The following Monday, we started planning Split Rock's move to the Twin Cities, where, beginning in 2004, we would have beautiful painting, drawing, printmaking, and fiber arts studios courtesy of the University's design department.

*

By 2005, seven punishing years after Tom's death, I was no longer a decade away from retirement. An eternity, spent inside a walled fog without seasons or sunrises or menstrual periods, had passed. Miraculously, I was only two years shy of my sixty-second birthday. Even better, in just twenty-one months, the sum of my age and my years of University employment would total ninety. At that point, I would become eligible to retire early and collect my full pension, the same amount I would be paid if I were to wait until age sixty-five to retire. In just twenty-one more months, I could liberate myself, assuming that I could afford to retire and assuming that I could tough it out for two more years. Of that I was not sure, to say the least.

Then, out of the blue, I was given the gift that would ulti-mately allow me to once again take pleasure in my work. Like the rest of our country's population, CCE's audience was aging. For decades, we had served Minnesota's baby boomers, first by enabling them to earn degrees, and then through life-long learning and continuing education in their fields. But by 2005, many of these people were aging beyond their need for and interest in some of CCE's longest-running programs. In 2006, the country's seventy-six million baby boomers would begin turning sixty, and new, more relevant programs would be needed as they looked forward (or not) to transitioning away from full-time work and toward whatever postcareer life would become.

The baby boom was about to become a retirement boom. The possible effects of this demographic revolution on CCE did not go unnoticed by our dean, and she committed our unit to creating programming that would be newly relevant to our longtime audiences. She asked me to work with her to explore possibilities, identify those worth pursuing, and lead an effort to develop relevant, resonant programs spe-cially designed to serve a diverse audience of baby boomers. In my new role, I would informally report to the dean, but I would also continue to report to my department supervisor, since the dean intended that any programs that emerged from our work would be housed in Personal Enrichment Programs. Nevertheless, a hierarchical barrier had been broken, some-thing with which the dean seemed perfectly comfortable, but Austen did not. By then, it was an old story. Still, I wanted to try to live with it. At long last, I was feeling energetic about my work. I knew I was climbing a high learning curve, but I was grateful for every vertical step.

Never had I imagined that I, who had been steeped in the arts for four decades, would begin learning why people retire and why they do not, why it is incumbent on us to make a positive difference in our world before we leave it, what to expect as our bodies age, how to preserve and enhance our physical and emotional well-being as we get older, what it means to have "enough," how to stay engaged in the adventures of life after one's career ends, how to stay intellectually acute throughout later life, and how to cultivate resilience as our losses accrue. I learned and learned and learned, and through that learning, I relearned the very lesson I sought to teach others: never stop learning. As humans, we rely on continuity to ground us, but we need novelty to grow and thrive.

Two programs emerged from our work: LearningLife, which became the University's signature collection of lifelong learning opportunities in the liberal arts, and Encore Transitions, a groundbreaking series of four daylong sessions that introduced a holistic approach to helping people prepare for a fulfilling postcareer life. To shape Encore Transitions, I collaborated with a family physician I had met at a seminar on encore careers, a newly coined term at the time. Under the aegis of a midcareer fellowship, he was exploring similar programming for physicians to help address late-career burnout. Together we created a broadly relevant series about aging well, including navigating the transition away from full-time work, maintaining and enhancing health and well-being, and giving to one's community through various forms of civic engagement.

Rather than simply blessing or nixing our work, my dean, who loved ideas and was a superb strategist, was also an active participant in our collaboration. But, like a dandelion in a field of clover, another problem was sprouting. Though I was spending more and more time working with the dean, I continued to report to Austen, so for all intents and purposes, I was serving two masters. From offering progress reports to making resource requests to seeking advice, I did each task twice, sometimes to differing, even opposing responses. This cumbersome arrangement consumed too much of my time, and it did not take long before Austen's growing resentment swelled into an outright cold shoulder.

Finally, after months of frustration, I spoke to the dean about my discomfort. I asked if we could formalize our working arrangement. I would report directly to her, and I would move into an office in her suite, which was one floor below my office in Personal Enrichment Programs. This she approved without argument or compromise; I think she understood that the situation had become untenable. I took an office that abutted the men's bathroom, the first in a row of offices that housed CCE's financial staff. No one saw whether I was in my office or not, and when I was there, no one except the dean cared what I was doing. That was how, one year before I planned to retire, I got my work groove back.

The chance to keep learning, create new programs, and meet and work with people outside the arts, including community activists, physicians, psychologists, politicians, volunteer coordinators, financial planners, and social services workers, literally breathed life into my days. Can meaningful work done in a tolerant workplace with compassionate colleagues help us heal from even our most profound losses? I hope it can. I imagine it can. I believe it can. Still, I will never know whether my newly found happiness at work was helping me emerge from my deepest grief or whether the grip of my now timeworn grief was weakening under its own weight, freeing me to embrace my work with renewed enthusiasm. It probably does not matter. All I knew was that I was beginning to surface, to lift my head above water.

PART II
SURFACING

7

The Music Lives

IF YOU HAVE EVER had the pleasure of driving across the Great Plains as they steadily gain altitude and give way to the foothills of the Rocky Mountains, you may have found yourself making gradual turns that are so wide you are not aware that you are changing direction. After an hour or two or three, it finally dawns on you that having spent the entire morning driving south, you are now going west. Recognizing your inattention, you are suddenly aware that the sun has crossed the road and the silhouette of the distant landscape has turned to muted purple peaks. Only then do you fully realize what has happened, and it delights you.

After seven years of acute grieving, I think that I experienced what I would now characterize as a subtle, wide turn in which pessimism, my constant companion for so long, was gradually giving way to an increasing willingness to accept reality. It was a surrender of sorts, as though my grief were

a resistant bacteria that had finally met its conquering antibiotic. I think I began to slowly awaken from an extended
limbo, a protracted, timeless time during which I was, as the
late Townes Van Zandt sang, "waiting around to die." It
was an unintentional, unconscious shift, since I had still not
regained my pre-fissure self-awareness, nor did I leap from
pessimism to optimism, as though that transformation were
binary: if you are not one, you must be the other. What I
experienced was fragile and humble: a renewing interest in
and openness to others, a soft but warming attraction to the
artistic and intellectual pursuits that had always enlivened me,
and even though my health was inexorably deteriorating, a
lifesaving interest in my new University work.

Tiny increment by tiny increment, I think my inner attention was moving from the dull stasis of prolonged grief over
Tom—missing him, yearning for him, dreaming that he
returned or never left, longing for life as it had been, feeling
separated from the living world—to the ultimately inescap-
able business of endeavoring to live without him. Though I
was not conscious of it, I must have reached a point where
trying to live seemed easier than trying to die: it may have
become the path of least resistance. At the same time, I still
felt wedded to Tom, I still loved him with all my heart, I still
felt him with me. I still found it too painful to look at photographs of him or conjure his body or his voice or reminisce
about him, but I believe that I must have been moving toward
a more peaceful, sane way of living without and with him, if
one can imagine such a coexistence.

By coexistence, I do not mean continuing to live with one
foot in the grave, as I had done for seven years, nor do I mean
living with one arm reaching for heaven, as Michelangelo's

Adam does to this day. In life and death, Tom had always been an unforgettable presence in my life, and now I was beginning to imagine myself reentering the world without leaving him behind. It was this fragile, partial reconciliation that would help me pave a path to healing, however long and winding. To think of Tom as purely a memory would have been impossible. I could not have relegated him to such a distant status, especially considering that my memories of him were still so painful as to be inaccessible. Nor could I have transformed him into a proverbial angel on my shoulder, a cheerful cherub watching over me. These compartments may have efficacy for others, but I had not stopped feeling Tom's presence. He was neither memory nor angel to me. As time went on, his continuing presence, the same presence that had long driven my grief, was now helping me feel more content and better able to live the earthly life to which I awoke each morning.

In that earthly life, I also could not imagine replacing Tom with a different husband. For some women who are widowed in midlife, remarriage may be a healthy step as they recover from grief or a natural step after they have recovered. It may help some widows settle their grief and leave their mourning behind, but the thought of emotional bigamy felt unendurable to me. The truth is that marriage for its own sake never suited me. I had crushes in high school, and I dated, sometimes reluctantly, through my twenties. I had genuine friendships and warm professional relationships with good, interesting men, but I never fell in love with any of them. After all, I was an introvert, and that made me (perhaps too) particular about friends and lovers. I did not and do not trust easily. I married in my early thirties only when I found myself head over heels in love. Once Tom died, I had no thought that lightning could or would strike twice. I still felt bound to him, I still felt married, and though the character of my grief seemed to be moderating and its power over my life loosening, my love for him remained constant, steadfast, and enduring. Death cannot kill love.

*

For years, I had been searching for ways to serve developing writers and artists who did not have access to arts learning in their homeplaces, and finally, with the advent of web-based platforms, I was able to work with our technologists to do so. I created a program called Online Mentoring for Writers (OMW). Of all the programs I developed at the University of Minnesota, OMW was one of the most valuable. Using a wholly online system, it enabled English- and Spanish-language poets, fiction writers, and writers of literary non-fiction to work one-on-one with experienced writer-teachers without the exigencies of email. OMW was flexible for both parties and provided mutual accountability. Our teacher-mentors were renowned and respected, and they were dedicated to this way of learning.

As far as I know, OMW was the first program of its kind in the United States, and it fulfilled its unique promise beautifully. We served writers from every continent on Earth. Our clients ranged from military personnel to over-the-road truck drivers to wheelchair-bound writers to Peace Corps and Vista volunteers to prisoners and busy business people. Importantly, the program was private: no one saw clients' writing except their mentors, and there was no peer feedback, something that had long rankled some participants in Split Rock's workshops. After all, your "peers" may not necessarily be your peers.

On its public-facing side, our web-based client-mentor interface worked reasonably well, but behind the veneer, the software was an unpredictable, illogical, Rube Goldbergesque black hole. The developer who built the system was careless and the prelaunch testing insufficient, so the system was in constant need of repair and revision. Saddled with maintaining this gargoyle was our unit's first-ever webmaster, a young man whom I will call Ned. I first met Ned in our marketing department's breakroom, where we were both silently observing a large box of Krispy Kreme doughnuts that someone had set on the counter. I started the conversation. "They're very consistent, aren't they?"

"Yes," Ned said. "They're very consistent." We each took one, and that was how I first met Ned.

Because of the never-ending need to diagnose and correct OMW system issues, Ned and I saw each other frequently. I would bring him problems, and after running through an array of possible errors and malfunctions, he would jury-rig solutions. One afternoon, while visiting Ned's cubicle, I noticed a compact disc on the shelf above his desk. It was a double album called *Live at the Old Quarter, Houston, Texas* by someone named Townes Van Zandt, a name I had never heard before. Given the title of the album and the cowboy hat on the head of the man pictured on its cover, I assumed that Townes Van Zandt must be a country singer. Though I had not listened to music in seven years, I picked up the CD and took a look at the list of songs. To my astonishment, one of them was "Pancho and Lefty," one of my all-time favorite songs. As a devoted fan of Emmylou Harris, I had listened to it countless times; it was one of her signature songs. But in the twenty-five years I had known that song, I had never bothered to find out who wrote it. Lo and behold! It was the artist I would come to know as the late great Townes Van Zandt.

I asked Ned if I could borrow the CD, and that afternoon, without thinking, I casually inserted it into my car player and listened to it during my drive home from work. It did not unleash a crying jag, it did not bite me, it did not make me ache or set me to yearning. Purely and simply, it was music to my ears. After seven soundless years, all it took was the right song at the right time to restore my capacity to enjoy music. At last, I could be moved! How could such a miracle have happened so offhandedly? So unexpectedly? Still fresh in my memory was the musical ambush I suffered a month after Tom died. It happened while I was in Walgreen's buying toiletries. Background music was playing in the background, but I was not paying attention to it: I simply wanted to buy what I needed and leave. But when the song changed to "Always on My Mind" by Willie Nelson, my throat tightened, my tears welled up, and I croaked out a cry. An uncontrollable crying jag was coming, and I was powerless to stop it. I put down my items and rushed out of the store.

Now, out of the blue, my fear of music seemed to have passed. A part of me seemed to have been repaired: how and why seemed unimportant. That weekend, I lugged my stereo equipment up from the basement, connected the necessary cables, attached the speaker wires, and began listening to some of my record albums. I was not ready to listen to the doo-wop songs that Tom and I used to dance to in our living room, but I felt like a newborn as I listened to my favorite Ry Cooder songs, especially "Women Will Rule the World" and "Jesus on the Mainline"; my favorite Emmylou Harris songs, especially "Boulder to Birmingham" and "Before Believing";

my favorite Joan Baez songs, especially "Be Not Too Hard" and "Joe Hill"; and my favorite John Prine songs, especially "Hello in There" and "Sam Stone."

The following week, Ned and I got to talking, and I mentioned that I had a library of about six hundred vinyl record albums that I had been collecting since high school. His eyes lit up: "Can I come and see them?"

"Sure," I said. "Why not!"

That weekend, Ned and I partook of the plethora of geniuses residing in my music library, including Junior Walker and the All Stars, Los Lobos, Mahlathini and the Mahotella Queens, Professor Longhair, the Roches, and Etta James. At last! Now, having been reborn, I was thirsty, and my record albums, cassette tapes, and compact discs were not enough. As I had throughout my life, once again I craved music that was new to me, like the beautiful songs of Townes Van Zandt.

There was only one solution. I had to purchase an updated iMac computer so that I could download the iTunes application from Apple. My current iMac was almost six years old, and I had deliberately postponed replacing it because I was reluctant to spend the money until it was absolutely necessary. Thanks to Townes Van Zandt, it was now necessary. Luckily, University staff received a discount on home computers from our bookstore, so the deed was quickly accomplished. Readers who remember the original advertisements for the iMac will remember that Apple claimed that the computer could be fully set up by a seven-year-old boy and his dog. That gave me confidence. On May 12, 2005, I downloaded my first song from iTunes, "Blinded by the Light" by Bruce Springsteen. That was followed by 2,800 more songs over the next fourteen years, some of which I have just called upon to nourish this writing.

Not only did I savor the listening, I was also attracted to the learning. I had always taken pleasure in learning about the music and artists I loved, and now I wondered about Townes Van Zandt, who had died a year before Tom at age fifty-two, the same age as Tom when he died. Ned was also a dedicated fan, so he and I decided to pool our resources in order to obtain Townes's complete recorded works, fifteen albums in all. Since Ned already owned one CD, each of us bought seven CDs. We then loaned them to each other so that we could upload them to our iTunes libraries. In this way, we were each able to acquire Townes's entire oeuvre.

I could now listen to most of the music I loved. I knew where my heart lay, even though it had been almost eight years (a minute? an eternity?) since I had seen Tom's face, held him in my arms, kissed his lips, and heard his soft voice. Time creates distance, but memory collapses time. Still, I was not ready to put that belief to a test. I was living on while my memories continued to lie in wait, anticipating a time, perhaps many years away, perhaps never in this lifetime, when they would no longer bring me pain.

*

Though I have never witnessed a melting glacier, I have always been electrified by the spectacular sight of gigantic chunks of blue ice sliding away from an iridescent glacial cliff, splashing into the water, and floating away on the summer sea. After reuniting with music, I began to feel like a newly released ice chunk, free to float in whatever direction the prevailing current took me. I think I know why. As my new programs became my primary focus at work, I unceremoniously detached myself from the Split Rock Arts Program, the glacier that had defined my work for over twenty years. That emotional distance helped me realize a grand irony: Split Rock had squelched my creativity. The creative energy I gave to the program left me sapped because it arose from the same source—the same part of my being—as my energy for making art. Only recently, so long after the fact, has this become clear to me. The idea that Split Rock had somehow robbed me of my right to be an artist would have never crossed my mind while I directed the program.

Out of a self-conceived ethic, I deliberately sacrificed my own art spirit to those of the artists whom we invited to teach at Split Rock. To work effectively with them, I felt that I needed to avoid falling into artist-to-artist relationships, which would have been not only inappropriate for someone in my role but a shameful assertion of my own needy ego. Instead, I tried to create administrator-to-artist relationships. Very few of the hundreds of artists and writers with whom I worked ever asked how I became conversant in their art forms. They rightly cared about their own creative work, about their students, and about ensuring that our published descriptions of their workshops would be accurate and complete. In telephone and in-person conversations with them, I focused on their creative processes, their views about the art forms in which they worked, their approaches to teaching, and their motivations. In this way, I learned discernment, coming to believe that the best artists are also the best people.

It was fulfilling work, but it subsumed my identity as an artist. Though I admit to being a willing conspirator, I also feel that it was something in the nature of the work, because after I stopped working with artists and writers, my creative spirit seemed to resurface. It was sparked by an invitation I received from the University's library system. Through my work with Ned, I had earned a narrow reputation as someone who was interested in social media, which was in its infancy in 2006. The library had recently launched a blogging platform called UThink, and every faculty member, staff member, and student at the University of Minnesota was given a blog space to use in whatever way we wished. Because of the sheer size of the University, UThink became, at birth, the largest blogging site in North America. Along with several colleagues, I was asked to write a blog and report on my "user experience" so that the University's blogmaster could monitor the system. There were no rules: I could name my blog anything I wanted and write anything I wanted as long as I remained civil.

In this accidental way, I began my vocation as an occasional essayist and amateur composer of verses. I named my blog *Randomly Andy* and set to writing my first essay, "Blogination, Blogtation, and Blogesty," a perplexing play on imagination, quotation, and modesty that even today serves as an awkward but appreciated reminder that once upon a time we were all beginners at something. A couple of months after I started writing, I knew that I needed something more than a collection of random ramblings. I craved a sweeping theme, something into which I could sink my metaphorical teeth.

I thought of Townes Van Zandt (heart attack, age fifty-two), Gram Parsons (drug overdose, age twenty-six), Frank Zappa (prostate cancer, age fifty-two), Janis Joplin (heroin overdose, age twenty-seven), Warren Zevon (mesothelioma, age fifty-six), and Bob Marley (melanoma, age thirty-six), and decided to embark on a project I called Musicians in Heaven. Here was a way for me to pay tribute to musicians whose work and lives intrigued me, and who, like Tom, had ascended to heaven before their time. I had written to serve my profession for so many years, I had taken my commitment to my University work so seriously, I had asked so much of art. Now, finally, I wanted only to take pleasure in acts of creation. I no longer wanted to worry about whether my efforts were serious enough, whether they carried enough social or political weight, or whether they evidenced "excellence."

I reveled in writing essays: I loved the way I could wander, letting one thought flow into the next and discovering what I wanted to say as I said it. That is the great gift of writing, and it is also the great gift of computers, which give our hands the ability to (almost) keep up with our minds. But I was not content. Soon after I began working on Musicians in Heaven, I decided that in addition to written tributes, I wanted to create visual tributes, since some of the musicians' stories seemed better suited to paintings or posters than to essays or poems. That is when I knew that I had to start painting again. Even more than recovering my love of music, returning to painting would be the deepest reawakening I had experienced since Tom died, but that did not occur to me at the time. The only thing on my one-track mind was my need to get my easel back from my friend Sherry.

For several years, Sherry had been suffering from debilitating chronic back pain, so she had been painting seated at a table. My easel had been relegated to her sister's garage, but long before that, Sherry's brother-in-law had cut six inches off its top so that it would fit in Sherry's low-ceilinged apartment. When I saw it covered in cobwebs and missing its crown, I felt almost as sad as the day I gave it to her. To say that I regretted having parted with it is an understatement, but at the time, I had assured her that I could never paint again. Its neglect and mutilation had been my own fault, but the fact that it had survived its eight-year absence from my life was enough to bring tears of gratitude to my eyes. I hauled it home, put on a pair of rubber gloves, and cleaned it up.

After that, I hiked up to the attic and brought down my painting supplies. I was amazed that some of my acrylic colors were still workable, and my brushes, some of which had been with me for thirty years, were intact and ready for duty. Then I made a trip to my neighborhood art supply store, which had not changed appreciably in eight years, gathered the colors I needed, treated myself to a few new brushes, and splurged on an eleven-by-fourteen-inch hardbound sketchbook, which has been my notebook, scrapbook, and drawing pad ever since.

*

Painting and writing for my own pleasure were the most powerful, sustained releases from paralyzing grief I had experienced since Tom's death. Imagine exhaling after holding your breath for almost eight years! There is a Yiddish word, *machaye,* that can mean relief from something that undermines your well-being and can also mean something that revitalizes or rejuvenates. Imagine that you are sitting on your front porch on a humid, ninety-degree August day. There is no wind: nothing is moving. The heat is stifling, the humidity worse. Then, as the long, still afternoon begins to give way to evening, you feel a small breeze graze your forehead. Within a few minutes, that tiny breeze, the harbinger of cooler, less steamy air, has turned brisk, drying your sweat and giving you new energy just in time for dinner. That is a *machaye.* A relief. To paint again! To write for pleasure! *Machayes!*

Being at one with an immersive endeavor of our own choosing transports us to a psychic place outside ourselves, where, for at least a while, we can forget everything except the activity at hand. Any all-consuming activity counts, whether it is painting a picture, writing a poem, sewing a quilt, reading a gripping novel, or building a lamp from a block of wood. After eight years of complicated grief, this unification of the doer with the doing helped liberate me from the unrelenting, insufferable self-preoccupation that had smothered me for so long. The ability to forget oneself in an activity outside the self is also one of human nature's most powerful medicines: it heals, it refreshes, it dissolves stress, it makes us happy. It is a *machaye*.

This state of humble bliss has been explored most famously by the psychologist Mihaly Csikszentmihalyi, who, as a productivity expert, studied creativity and happiness, observing and ultimately recognizing the state of being at one with an activity. He named it "flow." During my protracted time of intense grief, I had lost the ability to enter a state of flow. I was not able to psychically leave myself, which meant I had no respite from my grief. Even when reading a book, an escape method I had always taken for granted, I could not fully immerse, in part because grief is a bully: it viciously interfered with my ability to concentrate. I felt this absence acutely, and it tore at me, especially as year after year went by and I did not normalize.

I wonder now if this simple ability to lose ourselves in something outside ourselves is a mark of sanity, a way of saving ourselves when we can no longer recognize the person we have become, when we feel that our selfhood, the bounded concept that grounds us in the living world, has strayed beyond our grasp or betrayed us, preventing us from "getting hold of ourselves." That is how I felt during my time of prolonged grief. Only now do I recognize that once I began to take pleasure in pleasurable activities, I felt myself coming home, reuniting with the person who genuinely enjoyed life most of the time and could weather difficulties and disappointments.

8

Moving Out, Moving In

IN JULY 1982, when Tom and I bought our home, Ronald
Reagan was president of the United States, annual mortgage
interest rates were 15 percent, and the fourplex in which we
were living was infested with giant cockroaches. Those were
our reasons for choosing a one-owner, one-bedroom bunga-
low in a safe, quiet St. Paul neighborhood. The house may
have been small, but the backyard was expansive: we reckoned there would be plenty of room for a good-sized addition, and there was. Twelve years later, after adding a bedroom and expanding our kitchen, we still had a backyard big
enough for a rollicking game of croquet. The front yard was
a different story. In 1924, a year after our home was built,
its owners, the childless Alma and Ferdinand Engfer, added
four feet to the front of the house, which meant that the row
of four front windows in our living room was only about six
feet back from the sidewalk.

Like many homes of its era, ours had lots of windows, but

because it was situated so close to our next-door neighbor's home, it was dark. If we opened our blinds, everything in our living room, including us, could be seen from the sidewalk, but that was a tiny price to pay for an inviting, comfortable dwelling perfectly suited to two people in love. Tom loved our little house, and I loved living in it with him. We planted a bountiful vegetable garden, Tom installed an appealing slatted privacy fence, and I sewed curtains for our kitchen on my mother's treadle-operated Singer. A natural putterer, Tom kept the house shipshape, and I cooked dinner every Sunday except during the summer, when Tom grilled chicken breasts or hamburgers on our bachelor-sized Weber grill.

Our corner lot was bordered on the east and west by opulent hedges of sumptuous lilacs. In May, when they bloomed, the scent was pervasive and rapturous: we used to lie on the grass in the backyard and breathe through our noses. Each Halloween, Tom carved a jack-o'-lantern, which we set on a table on our screened-in porch. One year, we decided to leave the pumpkin on the porch as a post-Halloween decoration. As it decayed, its face curled and wrinkled until it looked for all the world like an organic bust of Ronald Reagan. It was the hit of the neighborhood. Tom was also the hit of the neighborhood during the winter, when, after finishing our driveway and sidewalks, he would clear our neighbors' pavements with his trusty snowblower.

Though what I have just written is true, it sounds like a fairy tale: too good to last. It was, of course. We had our good and bad times, but our love for each other was constant and carried us through whatever difficulties we faced, which, when seen through the dust of decades gone, were not as trying as they seemed at the time. Two union strikes (including

one during which Tom served as a negotiator), a sprained
ankle, three cases of the flu, a sinus infection, two historic
blizzards, a stalled car, a flat tire, two power outages, a broken
washing machine, an electrocuted refrigerator, a frozen water
line: these were our trials until Tom's cancer diagnosis. While
he was sick, home maintenance projects were postponed, but
we discussed in detail the projects he wanted me to take care
of after he died. I have no doubt that his mind was eased
knowing that he could trust me to carry out his wishes, and I
am sure that he never doubted I would do so.

For the first few years after Tom died, I continued to love
our house. It was the place where he was most present to me,
it was the place where our love continued to live, and should
he transcend death, it was the place to which his soul would
return. The trouble was that my day-to-day life in the house
had deteriorated. I no longer felt safe there. I kept the blinds
drawn day and night. I locked every window every night, so
nighttime breezes never freshened our rooms. There was a
glassless gap in one of our basement windows where Tom
had installed the vent for our clothes dryer, and every time I
looked at it, I felt like a sitting duck. I thought about hiring
someone to seal it, but I had no idea how to find the right
person, and lacking the focus to think it through, I postponed
it, along with most of the rest of our home maintenance items.

Then, one day about a year after Tom died, I found a letter
in our mailbox. It was not postmarked; it had been dropped
there by its sender. Its sender was a neighborhood boy who
was writing to ask whether he could use our house as a fort.
The house, enclosed in Venetian blinds and in dire need of
paint, must have given the boy the impression that it was
uninhabited. Thankfully, that was enough to move me to get

the house painted. A few months later, our old furnace, which had been a workhorse since 1955, died. It was only when the new one was being installed that I discovered that Tom had blocked the heat to our bedroom. Up until then, all I knew was that after I started sleeping alone, I was so cold that I bought a space heater, which I used every night. A year or so after the furnace conked out, our plumbing finally crumbled, and I had to spend eight thousand dollars to replace it.

With Tom bodiless, the only human activity in our basement occurred when I did laundry, so our centipede population, which had always frightened and revolted me, grew. Not only did the number of centipedes grow, the centipedes themselves grew larger. I used to see a centipede in our bathroom or kitchen a few times a year; now I saw them every few weeks. I was no longer comfortable walking barefoot, I had to check the bathtub every day, and when I did have to kill one, it gave me the shivers for hours. These encounters so afflicted me that I had frequent nightmares about them for years.

There I was, still wedded to the home Tom and I knew and loved together. I thought of moving almost every day, but I was terrified that leaving our home would mean leaving him. The case against staying was elephantine: I no longer felt safe there, maintenance and repair were devouring my savings, and I could not do any of the routine maintenance myself, whether mowing the lawn, clearing the snow, or changing from screened windows to storm windows and back again in the fall and spring. I was afraid of the bugs, and the unbroken darkness was oppressive. Leaving was probably inevitable, but without our home as our North Star, would Tom be able to find me? Would we be severed from each other forever?

*

Today, when visitors enter my condominium for the first time, they immediately exclaim over its abundant natural light. The impact is dramatic because my tiny foyer is dim, so when you enter, it takes a moment to realize that you are walking into a light bath created by the glass panes of the (almost) floor-to-ceiling windows on my condo's west and north sides. The condo is in the northwest corner of the fifth (and highest) floor of my building, making it perfect for watching sunsets, thunderstorms, and blizzards. In the summer, I call it my crow's nest, and in the winter, I call it my snow globe. My backyard is the Mississippi River, where, three seasons of the year, I can watch oversize barges carrying huge loads of unidentifiable cargo to unknown destinations. My front yard is the railroad track, where I can watch black tankers carrying natural gas and white tankers carrying milk from east to west and west to east all day long. Housed under the same roof as my condo are a Caribou Coffee restaurant and a gym called Anytime Fitness because it is open to members from early morning to late at night.

When I moved into my condominium in October 2007, I began living in a place where no one had ever lived. Everything in it was new: appliances, plumbing, fixtures, wiring. It was, for the time being, maintenance-free. It was also safe and private: at night I could leave the shades up and the windows open. Within days after I moved, I was sleeping more peacefully. The only bugs were the teeny spiders I would occasionally see on the window sills during the summer. I had trustworthy, tolerant neighbors, and there were no children searching for forts. Above all, I literally emerged from darkness into light. Adequate light is crucial to well-being. In a light environment, the conscious body feels lifted, more content, more optimistic, happier. When the body feels lifted, the spirit will follow, and the darkness within me, the shroud of grief that had cloaked me for over nine years, seemed to yield almost immediately after I moved. In a place like mine, expressly built to admit light, darkness could never dominate, and besides, I no longer had the will to resist. I surrendered to the sun.

Compared with our home, the condo was small. Our house had not only its main floor but a basement, an attic, and a garage, so before I moved I had to donate or otherwise dispose of twenty-five years of Tom's and my material lives, from the recliner in which he died to his weight bench and fishing equipment, and from my drawing table to my thirty-year-old darkroom equipment and two-thirds of my library. The process was gut-wrenching. My realtor called it "decluttering," but it was actually depersonalizing, dismantling, and destroying what had once been our home and leaving in its stead an inanimate, empty shell.

Of all the grim duties that fell to me after losing Tom, the undoing of his tangible life—the material evidence that he had lived—was the most heartbreaking. Until I sold our house, I had thought that nothing could have been harder than sorting through his clothing and personal notions, and donating or throwing away everything except the few items with which I knew I could never part: his orange western-style vest, his cowboy boots, his cutoff jeans, his Australian outback hat, and his billfold, which he had made himself from a kit.

One suffers myriad forms of torture as a grieving widow, but discarding one's husband's intimate personal effects is one of the worst. A month after Tom died, I followed my brother Bob as he drove Tom's two-year-old Dodge truck to the dealership from which we bought it. I looked into the manager's eyes as he handed me a check for more than the truck's value, and I drove Bob home without breaking down. Nine years later, I filled a garbage bag with Tom's shaving supplies, his mustache grooming kit, his headbands, his flip-flops, his baseball caps, his wrist protectors, his clogs, and his well-worn, beloved bathrobe, walked it out to our trash can, and deposited it as though it were the day's garbage. If, today, I was forced to discard the small collection of Tom's things that rest peacefully on my closet shelf, I have no doubt that I would suffer as intensely now as I did then. Time takes us only so far, and the rest is eternal.

After all that, and after too many years of believing that I could never leave our home, I had finally reached the point where I had no choice but to dispose of everything that could not move with me to my condominium. The process felt ruthless, disregarding as it did any modicum of sentiment and any recognition that some objects were fraught and carried the weight of a quarter-century. The items that the two college boys economically piled into the 1-800-GOT-JUNK? truck were not junk at all but the shards of once-whole effects that would now be irretrievably lost to time. To me, they may as well have been diamonds.

On the day I closed on the sale of our house, my condo was not yet ready, so I was staying with Nan and Allen. Perhaps because I was no longer living in the house, or perhaps because I was feeling such intense, surging grief, I forgot to turn over my house keys to the buyers. The day after the closing, I returned "home" to drop off the keys. As was my habit, I entered through the back door and into the kitchen, where the young couple who had bought the house were waiting, along with the young man's father. In the living room, the young woman's father and uncle were already at work pulling up the carpet. The feeling that I was a visitor, even a stranger, in my own home was so discomforting that I had difficulty holding back my tears during that five-minute stay. Our interaction in the kitchen was so cordial, so matter-of-fact, so unceremonious, that I felt like I was having an out-of-body experience. Worst, I knew Tom's heart was shattering.

Over the twelve years that I have lived in my condominium, I have had more than two dozen dreams about our house. In almost all of them, I am with Tom, either because he has returned to me during the dream or because he never left. In a few of them, I have returned to our house years later to find him still living there. In some of them, I return to our house, and while I am there, he pays me a visit. When I ask where he lives, he tells me that he has been living in an apartment on Saint Clair, a nearby street. I have had a few dreams in which he visits me at my condo, and together we return to our house. In almost all of my dreams about our house, someone else is living there, and we sneak in, only to worry that we will be discovered when the new owner comes home. In two or three of them, Tom has recovered from cancer, and we have remained in our home. In one of those dreams, he has recovered, but he is slightly disabled and walks with a cane.

Three months before he died, Tom had a cataract removed from his right eye, but that was as "old" as he ever got. Who, then, is the Tom who visits me in my dreams? Where has he been between visits? Why has he not grown older, like me? Perhaps, in my dreams, I am not my older self, the woman who is now more than twenty years older than he is. Perhaps I am stuck at fifty-three, just as he is frozen at fifty-two. How, then, in the distance between heaven and Earth, have we been able to keep abreast of each other? How have we managed to feel close to each other? Or have we? In the light of day, are such thoughts part of a grievous daydream in which I imagine that our relationship has simply continued as though it had never been interrupted? However unintentional, however beyond reason, that is how I feel after dreaming of him. It is unsettling, even now.

Prolonged, complicated grief not only impairs your reasoning; it disrupts your powers of self-observation. You no longer bother to notice yourself. Did my movement through life stop, at least in my mind, when Tom died? I know that physically, I moved through my days, but as I did so, I was not aware that I was getting older. I must have been aware of my birthdays, but I must not have associated them with the physical facts of aging that accompany the passage of time. I remember moments from my journey into menopause: the excruciating cramps during the last year or so of monthly ovulation, soaking a tampon every fifteen minutes in the ending throes of menstruation, and eventually, sometime (six months? a year?) after Tom died, entering menopause. There must have been other changes, too, some subtle, some glaring, but I was blind to them. Even today, almost halfway through the eighth decade of my life, I survey my body and wonder when all these changes happened. When did my skin become marked with freckles, bumpy blotches, and random red dots? When did I start bruising so easily? When did my hair start turning gray? When did it start thinning? How long have I had a bunion? When did my face turn old?

9

Defying Death

DURING THE DECADE after Tom's death, I had endured my grief problem, my smoking problem, my computer problem, and my supervisor problem, but in the end, it was my pooping problem that overtook them all. As luck would have it, I was born with a sensitive gut. I spent most of my life vacillating between constipation and diarrhea, and my symptoms worsened as I got older. As a young woman in my twenties, when I would try to ask a (male) doctor about my "stomach problems," I would be told that I had a "nervous stomach" and I should try to calm down. I felt too embarrassed to share the details that might have made a diagnosis possible, and I was never asked for more information about my symptoms. Because "generalized" symptoms like mine were presumed to be "female problems," they were dismissed as psychosomatic. Not once did a doctor suggest further examination in order to make a diagnosis.

By the time I reached my thirties and forties, I had learned to adapt my lifestyle to my ornery digestive tract, but this became more difficult as my work days became more demanding: two, three, and even four long meetings in a day, early meetings that meant that I had to leave for work before I could fully empty my bowels, and frequent daylong trips to Duluth that took two and a half hours each way and offered only one too-busy rest stop over the 150-mile journey.

Tom's favorite summer vacations were camping in the woods and on the shores of the lakes of northern Minnesota, and for several years, we took two or three camping trips each summer. We visited many of our state's most beautiful parks, exclaiming over spectacular lakeside sunsets, lying on our backs to gaze at dazzling night skies teeming with stars, and listening to astounding twilight loon concerts, sometimes with as many as twenty loons calling and responding on a shimmering lake. Along with these splendors, there were the thunderstorms that broke our sleep and left our campsite a muddy mess, the battalions of outsized mosquitoes that ate me alive but left Tom untouched, and the putrid outhouses that made me so nauseated, I could not sit long enough to move my bowels.

I always seemed to get my menstrual period during a camping trip, which never failed to exacerbate my bowel problems. During my most memorable example of this, a hot, humid sojourn at Glacial Lakes State Park in western Minnesota, my period was accompanied by profuse diarrhea, which meant that I had to sit in a daddy-longlegs-infested outhouse for an hour at a stretch nursing the ninety-one mosquito bites I suffered on that trip. I felt as though I would die and might well have done so had we not left that tick-ridden mosquito land in the nick of time. I encased myself in calamine lotion, and Tom drove the three hours home. At eleven o'clock that night, I ran an Aveeno bath and soaked until my nerve endings quieted. After drying myself, I dabbed calamine on my bites, counting them as I went along, and compelling a sympathetic but tuckered-out Tom to dab and count the ones on my back. That was our final camping trip; I simply could no longer endure the exigencies of the wild.

By getting up very early in the morning (for most of us, the middle of the night) and arriving at my office later and later as time went on, I was able to spend enough early-morning time at home to move my bowels several times. For a long time, this habit enabled me to carry on at work in relative comfort. Then, soon after Tom died, my symptoms worsened precipitously. My daily bowel movements doubled from about six to about twelve each day, and some days I defecated fifteen times. Imagine that you are dressed and ready to leave home for the day. Your car keys are in hand; your handbag is over your shoulder. Then, as you open the back door, you have a sudden, urgent need to move your bowels. You hurry to the bathroom, where you sit on the toilet for fifteen or twenty minutes. As nature takes its course, you contemplate what excuse you will make for your tardiness. Now, imagine this sequence repeating itself three or four times each week.

Because I had no diagnosis—no medical explanation to validate a claim of illness as my reason for tardiness or absence—and because it was impossible for me to enter a meeting or my office suite and cheerily announce, "Gosh, I'm sorry! I was having an especially long episode of diarrhea this morning," I was considered a slacker who was trying to worm her way out of doing a day's work. At that time, my office was located off a small exit hallway, and on more than a few occasions, I was able to sneak out of the office, drive home, release a deluge of diarrhea, drive back to campus, and resituate myself in my office without being noticed. Colleagues, including my supervisor, who stopped by to see me simply assumed that I was elsewhere in the building.

For years, my then doctor tried to diagnose what was becoming a significant disability. At the time, preventative-care colonoscopies were not yet the norm, and for reasons that remain unclear to me, she did not recommend a diagnostic one for me. Instead, I underwent two flexible sigmoidoscopies that showed nothing out of the ordinary. She also prescribed two different medications, neither of which helped, and finally suggested that I take Imodium, an over-the-counter antidiarrhea drug, which helped a little, but constipated me if I took it too often. That constipation would usually be broken by extreme, dehydrating diarrhea, which left me with a stinging, sore rectum, sometimes for days on end. As if this were not enough, my digestive problems seemed to worsen whenever I got a cold. My immune system was already compromised because of my emphysema, and I was catching severe colds every three or four months that kept me away from my job for several days at a time. My doctor preferred to treat separate conditions separately, and she was not willing to consider a connection between my digestive problems and my emphysema, even though it was crystal clear to me that one existed.

Finally, in early 2008, she sent me for a colonoscopy. It had taken her seven years to reach that decision. My persistent grief, by now my conjoined companion, coupled with my reluctance (stemming from embarrassment) to talk freely about my symptoms to friends, family, and co-workers, had so fogged my thinking that during all those years, it never occurred to me to get a second medical opinion. I unquestioningly assumed that there was no help for me, that this was something that ran in my family, and that it was part of a slow dying process.

*

My colonoscopy confirmed that I had Crohn's disease, from which, according to my newly acquired gastroenterologist, I had probably been suffering for most of my life. In my recovery-room consultation, he told me that my colon was so inflamed at the "terminal ileum," he could not insert his forceps high enough to take a tissue sample for biopsy. He recommended an immediate examination of my small intestine, and after that, a follow-up consultation with him. The terminal ileum is the place where one's small intestine meets one's large intestine, and it is the location that Crohn's disease loves most. If you were to take a pop quiz on the human digestive tract and you had no prior knowledge about it, you would probably never imagine that the so-called small intestine is about twenty feet long and the so-called large intestine is about five feet long. The nomenclature arises because the small intestine is only about an inch in diameter, whereas the large intestine is about three inches in diameter. Our intestines run from our stomachs to our rectums, but the word *colon* usually refers only to the large intestine.

A week after my colonoscopy, I went to the hospital for a "small bowel" examination, one of those dreaded procedures in which one is required to drink a solution of barium sulfate, a white liquid-like mixture similar to cement slurry. Once the concoction coats the digestive tract, the walls of the intestine are visible on a radiologic image. The pitiable patient drinks down about a cup of the barium as quickly as possible and then waits for it to coat the part of the digestive tract to be examined. Unfortunately for me, this was my terminal ileum, the lowest end of my small intestine, which meant that the barium solution had to travel down my esophagus, through my stomach, and through nearly twenty feet of bowel before it reached its destination. The attending nurse instructed me that walking helps speed the journey, so I obediently paced the hallways around the imaging laboratory. After an hour or so, the nurse laid me out on a glass table and fetched the radiologist, who was wearing multicolored sneakers. "Too bad," he said after a quick look at my insides. "The barium is only about halfway there."

"Oh, no!" I blurted in a high-pitched voice. I felt like Mr. Bill.

I was then given a cup of a stronger barium solution, which was a nauseous pale green in color. I paced for another forty-five minutes, and finally, the nurse called me. Once again, I was laid out on the glass table. As we were waiting for the radiologist, the nurse casually told me that I had the longest stomach she had ever seen. The radiologist took a look at my bowel and asked me if anyone had ever told me that I had Crohn's disease. "Yes," I answered. "My gastroenterologist told me that just last week." He then went on to explain that I had a stricture, or severe narrowing of my bowel, at my terminal ileum. From years of constant inflammation, scar tissue had built up on the walls of my small bowel near the ileum, narrowing its canal and increasing the likelihood of a bowel blockage. "All it would take is a chunk of steak," he warned. "See your doctor about surgery."

After more than half a lifetime, I not only had a diagnosis but was facing the prospect of surgery to remove two and a half inches of what the surgeon called "diseased bowel" near my terminal ileum. There are medications that can calm inflammation in Crohn's patients, but a stricture cannot be undone with drugs. Surgery is the only treatment. Unfortunately, it is accompanied by a major caveat: though the most diseased part of the bowel will be gone forever, the Crohn's disease will not. It will live on to attack again and again the part of the small bowel nearest the terminal ileum. Absent a way to permanently reduce the inflammation that hallmarks Crohn's, future surgeries will likely be needed.

I began a course of steroids, which I could not tolerate. I suffered a constant, unrelenting headache, I became unsteady when walking, and my blood pressure rose, a dangerous side effect because I was already taking medication for hypertension. By September 2009, when I finally had a "hemicolectomy" to remove the narrowed part of my intestine, the state of my health was deemed medically complicated. In fact, the surgeon required that before I could have surgery, I had to be examined by my pulmonologist to make sure that I could tolerate a general anesthetic. Thankfully, I came through the surgery without incident and was sent home to complete my recovery. I had been home for three or four days when I began to feel feverish, out of sorts, and exceptionally tired. I called my surgeon, who immediately sent me for a CT scan to determine whether my surgery site was infected. Abscesses are common after bowel surgeries, and sure enough, I had one. At four o'clock in the afternoon, I was sent directly from the imaging clinic to Regions Hospital in downtown St. Paul for intravenous antibiotics. Thus began what I can only call a near-death experience.

I was assigned to the third bed in a room originally meant for two patients. The hospital was in the midst of remodeling, but our room was in its old part. The room was filthy, dingy, and freezing cold. My bed was near the radiator, which, unsurprisingly, was stone cold. At my bedside was a hospital directory, so I took it upon myself to call the maintenance department and report a malfunctioning radiator. A workman arrived within a few minutes, proclaiming that the room felt like "room temperature" to him. Fortunately, my nurse had swathed me in heated blankets, so I managed to respond. "It's not room temperature. It's freezing in here. Too cold for sick people." That was enough to motivate him to take his wrench and fiddle with the radiator. Then he tackled the thermostat, and after a couple minutes of silent consideration, he turned to me and said, "Okay, I jacked it up to sixty-eight for you."

My nearest roommate was a young woman who had obviously been terribly injured. Her face and neck were covered in bruises, and her left arm, including her entire left hand, was wrapped in a thick bandage. Her bed was only about five feet from mine, so I could not help but overhear conversations at her bedside. The first of these was between two hospital staff women; one may have been a nurse. As the poor patient rested, awake but silent, the two confirmed to each other that the patient was scheduled for surgery the next morning to have her left hand rebuilt. Apparently, it had been crushed in a brutal beating she had received the night before at the hands of a boyfriend or husband. Shortly thereafter, two different women came to her bedside and began a conversation with her. Very quickly, I came to understand that one was a social worker and the other a translator: my roommate spoke no English, and her social worker spoke no Spanish.

Her heartbreaking story was that she had indeed been abused by her live-in boyfriend and was now suffering from the worst of the frequent beatings she had received at his hand. Somehow, she had managed to escape from their home and get to the emergency room, but her toddler daughter was still with him. She could not return to him: she feared for her life. "What will happen to my daughter?" she asked, and then, probably rhetorically, "Where will I go? I have no place to live." The social worker assured her that they would be sending child protection workers to get her daughter, and that she and her daughter would be placed together in a shelter where they would be safe. For now, she should not worry; she should just concentrate on her recovery. The social worker assured her that she was safe in the hospital. After this brief interview, the two left, promising to see her again the next day.

A few minutes later, a male nurse approached her bedside and asked if she wanted to go to the bathroom, a question she may not have understood. That was all I needed to hear. Sick though I was, nothing could have stopped me from calling him over, which I did politely but firmly. I told him that this woman needed a female nurse. I explained gently but clearly that she had just suffered a beating at the hands of her boyfriend and that the last thing in the world she needed was a male nurse taking her to the bathroom and helping her pull down her underpants. I knew he meant no harm, but the sheer thoughtlessness of assigning a male nurse to an abused woman was horrifying. He himself should have known better, even if his charge nurse did not. I asked him to send the charge nurse to see me.

She came within a minute or two, and I told her the same thing. She confessed that she had just come on duty and had not yet reviewed my roommate's chart, but agreed that it was inappropriate to have assigned her to a male nurse. Moments later, a soft-spoken young female nurse came to take my roommate to *el baño,* and having just taken my trazodone, I dropped off to sleep. When I awoke the next morning, my roommate had already been taken to surgery. I never saw her again.

After twenty-four hours of intravenous antibiotics and two nights in the hospital, my original symptoms seemed to have improved, but I knew that I was still not well. In fact, though I would not admit it to anyone but my sister Nan, I was actually feeling worse. Even so, I desperately wanted to go home, where I could heal. Hospitals are not places of healing. For many of us, they are places where we might actually get sicker, as I did during surgery when my intestines were lying flaccidly on my stomach fully exposed to the hungry bacteria hanging around in the operating room. I was still under my surgeon's care, so when he came to see me the following morning, I told him that I was going home to get well, adding that if he refused to discharge me, I would leave of my own accord. He sent me home with ten-day courses of two oral antibiotics, Bactrim and Flagyl, the same two I had been taking intravenously in the hospital.

Little did I know that I was allergic to both medications. That was why I left the hospital feeling unwell. By the time I was two days into the oral antibiotics, I was sicker than I had ever been in my life. I was running fevers as high as 103 degrees, I was throwing up all my meals, I was having unceasing diarrhea, I was dizzy, my ears were ringing loudly, my head felt like a vise, my mouth was parched, and I was too weak to wash myself. Even in such a state, I realized that I must be allergic to the antibiotics, and I was scared. I no longer trusted my surgeon, so I called my gastroenterologist, with whom I had a shocking conversation. He defended the surgeon's choices of antibiotics. "Well," he said, "you only have a few days left. Finish the antibiotics and then you'll start feeling better." It was obvious where his loyalty lay. In his zeal to support his colleague, he had misjudged my symptoms, which I later learned were life-threatening. Needless to say, I never saw or talked with him again.

That night, lying sleepless and roiling in bed, I tried to think through what would happen if I stopped taking the antibiotics. Did I prefer to die of an abdominal abscess? Or would I rather die of allergic reactions to antibiotics? Here was my train of thought: (1) I already had taken the antibiotics for four days, two in the hospital and two at home. That, I reasoned, was probably enough to kill the infection. (2) I had nowhere to turn. I had failed to convince both my surgeon and my gastroenterologist that I was suffering and needed immediate help. (3) If I continued the antibiotics, I felt certain I would die. (4) Whatever the consequences, I would stop taking them.

The next morning, anger set in. I threw away the antibiotics. Coincidentally, a few minutes after that, my sister Nan called me to say that Allen, my scientist brother-in-law, had just consulted with a physician colleague, an infectious disease (ID) specialist, and he strongly recommended that I call my surgeon and have him make an immediate appointment for me with an ID doctor. I called my surgeon, who called me back within a few minutes. (He must have been worried, I thought at the time, or he would not have called back so promptly.) I told him that I was allergic to the antibiotics and had discontinued them and that I wanted him to make an immediate appointment for me with an ID specialist. He retorted, saying that he did not think I needed an ID doctor, and recommended I return to the hospital. What? Head pounding, I told him that I was not going to the hospital and that he should make that appointment immediately. "I will not take no for an answer," I said stoically. He acquiesced.

The following day, I had a CT scan of my abdomen to see whether any infection remained. Following that, Nan accompanied me to an appointment with the infectious disease specialist. By then, I had not taken any antibiotics for thirty-six hours, and I was beginning to feel better. My symptoms were calming down: my fever had broken, I was no longer nauseated, and my head was no longer throbbing. I could feel that I was on the mend. The infectious disease specialist, a thoughtful, honest woman, reviewed both my CT scans: the one on which my infection was originally seen and the one taken that morning. She told me that my most recent scan showed no sign of infection, and that my earlier scan showed such a tiny area of infection that it would have probably resolved without antibiotics. She then updated my medical record to note allergies to Levaquin, Bactrim, Flagyl, and Amoxicillin.

For the first time in my life, I had been deathly ill and lived through it. No flu, no emphysema exacerbation, no sinus infection, no childhood disease, whether mumps, chicken pox, or measles, had ever approached the intensity of the physical distress I suffered while taking antibiotics to which I was allergic. It is deeply disturbing to me to think that I was voluntarily poisoning myself under doctor's orders. Importantly, I was alone in my condominium while doing this. There was no one to notice whether I was getting worse, no one to fear that I would become too sick to survive. There was no one to save me, especially if I had reached a point where I was too sick to save myself. Had I been inclined not to bother to save myself, there was no one to intervene, no one to shake that perverse inclination from me.

But at the time I was suffering, I never thought about my drawn-out wish to reunite with Tom. I did not consider the spiritual ramifications of my death. I thought only of death as a way to end my physical suffering. To live or die was not the question. The question was: what can I do to feel better, to end this horror? How remarkable it is that in the throes of acute illness, you forget the albatrosses that encircle your neck. You forget that you would like to die in order to be happy again. Such thoughts, even the most habitual, insistent ones, vanish in the face of acute physical suffering. Your thoughts, if you are able to think at such a time, begin and end with the state of your body. Then, when the suffering finally eases and you realize that the long-desired reunion had been much closer than you previously imagined, living begins to look more promising than dying.

When living begins to look more promising than dying, it finally occurs to you that through your own suffering, you have become a little less afraid to remember your husband's suffering. You have also learned more about the suffering of strangers, a lesson that your grief had kept from you. You are no longer obligated to imagine: you can feel it in your own memory. You begin to think outside yourself. You remember the young woman in the hospital and feel more acutely how she must have suffered at the hands of her boyfriend. You come to better appreciate the brevity of your own suffering and you begin to remember what it felt like to help others. You feel no shame for the attention you paid to your suffering; you simply start recovering your ability to live beyond it.

10

Health, Helping, and Healing

TWO MONTHS AFTER I moved to my condominium, Anytime Fitness opened its doors, and, in spite of my anxiety about the condition of my body, I joined the gym as an inaugural member. Other than riding my bicycle and hiking with Tom, I had not exercised regularly since playing volleyball in high school. I was almost as emaciated as celebrity bodybuilder Charles Atlas's "ninety-seven pound weakling," but now, having been a nonsmoker for almost a year, I felt that I had earned the right to try to become as physically fit as my damaged lungs permitted. Inaugural members were given one free session with a trainer, and that was how I met Mark, the trainer who helped me achieve a level of fitness that, given my severely diminished lung capacity, I never imagined possible.

From the beginning, Mark understood my body. He never put me in danger: he always found safe ways by which I could test and expand my limits. When I first started working with him, my limits were at once pitiful and mortifying. At our first session, he taught me two basic core-strengthening exercises: the forearm plank to strengthen the abdomen and the bridge to strengthen the lower back. I could hold the forearm plank for less than five seconds—really, just a blink or two of the eye—and I was so breathless by the time I caved in that I had to lie on my stomach for a minute or two to recover my breath. My first bridge went similarly: five seconds and plop. Along with core-strengthening exercises, Mark taught me how to use dumbbells, called "free weights" in fitness parlance, to strengthen my arm muscles and as handheld weights when doing squats and lunges to strengthen my leg muscles. He also taught me how to safely use the gym's array of training machines, which made me feel hip, like a person who knew what she was doing. It is a tribute to Mark that in two years of twice-weekly gym workouts, I never injured myself.

Had I realized exactly how deconditioned I was, I doubt that I would have had the temerity to join the gym, and not joining the gym may have amounted to an early death sentence, even though aging is not a disease unto itself. Nonetheless, as we get older and experience new health challenges, instead of actively caring for our bodies, many of us feel increasingly disassociated from our physicality. Over time, we tend to move less, which means that we become even less aware of the state of our bodies. As we move less, our desire to move continues to lessen, and we become caught in a vicious circle of decreasing body awareness and increasing immobility. But this scenario does not represent fate. There is plenty of credible research showing that many of the physical changes we attribute to "normal" aging are actually the result of inactivity. These changes are not inevitable, nor are they immutable. Our bodies are capable of restoration at any age.

In 2000, two years after Tom died, I was diagnosed with osteoporosis. My then doctor prescribed Fosamax, a bisphosphonate, to stabilize my bone loss and promote the growth of new bone. I took the drug religiously every Sunday for five years (the longest duration recommended by endocrinologists), but instead of improving over that time, my osteoporosis actually worsened. It was only after my Crohn's disease diagnosis that I learned that the body absorbs Fosamax at the terminal ileum, and because my terminal ileum was diseased, I never absorbed the Fosamax. To treat my osteoporosis with drugs, I would have to take them intravenously. Unfortunately, the intravenous osteoporosis drugs available at that time suppressed one's immune system for weeks after treatment. My immune system was already compromised because of my emphysema, so, with agreement from two endocrinologists, I decided against drug treatment. Having suffered three or four COPD exacerbations a year for several years, I did not want to tempt fate.

I did some homework and learned that weight-bearing exercise, from weight lifting to walking, can help build new bone. I also learned that improving one's balance skills can reduce the likelihood of falling. People with osteoporosis are at greater risk of breaking a bone if they fall, so preventing falls is, by itself, an efficacious treatment for osteoporosis. Separately, two good friends (both writers, but perhaps that does not matter) encouraged me to try yoga. They said it would get me moving, it included weight-bearing exercises, and it would help me improve my balance skills, which were nonexistent. Yoga? Me? A person who could hardly make it up a flight of stairs? I settled the question by demurring until, propitiously, the heavens smiled on me. After I had been working with Mark for about three months, Anytime Fitness began offering a yoga class for members. I was emboldened by then, so I thought, why not? I have nothing to lose. That was how I met Maren, who would be my primary yoga teacher and mentor for the next three years.

*

From the moment I came to yoga, I felt like a duck in water. It was the surprise of my life, and for good reason. I was a pudgy, awkward child who was forced at age four to take a class in tap dancing, ballet, and acrobatics from St. Paul's most revered dance teacher, Miss Dorothy Jean Mattimore. One of the "acrobatics" was a headstand, and to keep us safe, we wore hats made of two-inch-thick round discs of foam rubber. Alas, I was an ungainly hoofer, I could not balance on my tippy-toes, and even with my padded hat, I could not stand on my head. But there was a convincing reason for my lack of coordination: I had only one good eye. As I understand it, I was born severely nearsighted in my right eye (the good one), and I was so nearsighted in my left eye that it was pronounced functionally blind. I never stood a chance in Miss Mattimore's class.

One would think that because yoga teaches symmetry, having only one functional eye would be a prohibitive disadvantage, but that was not true for me. Of the many definitions one can find for the Sanskrit word *yoga*, the most common is "to unite" or "yoke," referring to the union of mind and body. When practicing a yoga pose (or yoga meditation or yoga breathing practices), the mind and body must behave as one, enabling the practitioner to achieve poise, balance, and alert comfort. On the mat, the imperfect mind can perfectly compensate for the imperfect body and vice versa. This means that we can achieve the same kind of satisfaction through yoga as is possible through any creative act, and, indeed, yoga felt like a creative process to me. Though I was on a mat, I felt the same pure pleasure as I did when painting at my easel. Each pose felt like a creation, the embodiment of an ecstatic process. Out of the blue, I had found another activity in which I could lose myself, travel away from my troubles, and be one with the moment.

Unfortunately, what my mind and body were actually doing stood in paradoxical contrast to the way I felt. First and foremost, I could not balance on one foot, so I was not able to hold classic balance poses like Tree (a one-footed standing balance done in television commercials on high peaks overlooking cavernous canyons), Warrior III (a forward bend from the hips done with one foot on the mat and the other leg lifted straight back behind the trunk so that it, the trunk, and the head are parallel to the ground), or Hand to Big Toe (in which the practitioner lifts one leg, bends the knee of the lifted leg, grasps the big toe of the lifted leg with the fingers of the same-side hand, and straightens the knee, thus extending the lifted leg straight forward from the hip). I fell out of these and other single-leg balance poses every time I attempted them: it was providential that I did not break a bone.

Still, under Maren's patient guidance, my classmates and I learned safe, gentle techniques for practicing yoga poses. I was relieved to discover that my fully sighted, healthy-lunged classmates experienced the same challenges as I did, and although I was the oldest member of the class (as I was in every yoga class I took), I could keep up with most of my classmates. Within a few weeks, I reached a point where I could remember how to do some of the poses we were taught, which enabled me to practice them at home. I also began buying books that pictured accomplished practitioners demonstrating poses. Those pictures not only helped me remember poses I had learned in class but enabled me to teach myself new poses. Even as I continued to learn from Maren, I began taking classes from other teachers, none of whom were as gifted as she was. After a year or so, I was taking two or three classes a week, but it was largely through a deliberate home practice, done alone at my own pace, that yoga became an integral part of my life.

My body welcomed yoga, and my mind was overtaken with it. Make no mistake: even with daily medication, I was limited by my emphysema. I could not do anything fast, and I could not repeat sequences of poses more than once or twice in succession. My teachers, while sensitive to me as an individual, were at least a generation younger than I was and had no experience teaching older students. I was coming to understand the obvious: that as we age, our bodies become more individualized and therefore less comparable to our contemporaries' bodies. Our journeys and genes have taken us in various directions, and those differences have imprinted themselves on our bodies. As I was learning more about how yoga worked, I was also teaching myself what I later came to call "age-appropriate, body-sensitive" approaches to poses and sequences. What is safe and comfortable for a thirty-year-old can feel like torture to a sixty-year-old. I have a longtime friend who once took a yoga class with a renowned "rock star" yoga teacher, and when I asked her what she thought of it, she said, "I thought I was going to die."

I was in a yoga frame of mind on a spring day in 2010, when I met my friend Bill, the physician with whom I was collaborating on Encore Transitions, at the Caribou Coffee restaurant in my condo building. He was preparing to leave town for a few weeks to treat people who were being sickened by the Deepwater Horizon oil spill in the Gulf of Mexico. His mission was sponsored by a humanitarian health organization to which he belonged, and as he talked about the volunteer opportunities this organization had afforded him, I began to realize that in my own life and work, I had never obtained skills that would allow me to directly help others, as Bill was doing. My skills were what people working in human resources would call "soft." True, I had developed educational programs that had helped the people they served, but I had no "hard" skills that I could employ in direct, face-to-face service to others. As I voiced this lament to Bill, it suddenly dawned on me—literally, in a flash—that I now had a skill: yoga. After all, I had two years of faithful practice under my belt. In that flash, I decided to train to become a yoga instructor.

Most yoga instructor training programs are offered through private, for-profit yoga studios, and they are expensive. For that reason, I turned to St. Paul's local community college, where I was able to take advantage of a state-mandated "senior citizen" discount on my tuition. At the instructor's invitation, I visited a class to observe her teaching and talk with her about how I might fare as an older trainee. She was encouraging, she was middle-aged, and her students were young and culturally diverse, all of which fed my enthusiasm. I applied, I was accepted, I endured the required appointment with an academic adviser, and I signed up for my first required course, Anatomy and Physiology, which was delivered online.

Thirteen days before the twelfth anniversary of Tom's death, on my sixty-fifth birthday, I was resentfully cramming for my final examination, fruitlessly trying to memorize the mechanics of human reproduction. Why in heaven's name would a sixty-five-year-old widow be reading a text designed for an eighteen-year-old practical nursing student? Because, as I came to realize over the coming months, I had entered a yoga instructor training program that had been developed on the cheap using the college's generic texts for health-related programs. Still, I persevered, suspecting that if the past was any prelude, I would mostly be teaching myself anyway. This, to my misfortune, would turn out to be only too true.

Our cohort of trainees spent eight hours in class two days each week for fifteen weeks. We did not meet in a studio but in a retrofitted training room in Henry Ford's Twin Cities assembly plant, located on a vast tract of land on a bluff above the Mississippi River. The plant, which had opened in 1925, had begun gradually shutting down in 2006, and by 2010 was renting its training rooms and some of its manufacturing facilities to the community college for its auto mechanic training program. Because it was no longer producing vehicles, the plant no longer maintained its physical facilities, and as autumn progressed, our classroom became chillier and draftier. By December, we had to wrap ourselves in blankets, and during our practice sessions, which were fewer and farther between as our classroom got colder and colder, our bodies were so chilled that we could not relax our muscles enough to do our poses properly. The result was that we were not given adequate training in executing and teaching yoga poses.

What did we do instead? During the warm weeks of early fall, we took long walks along the river bluffs, after which we descended multiple sets of steep steps to the river's bank, about thirty feet below street level. Once there, we were assigned ten-minute, fifteen-minute, and twenty-minute silent meditations, which most of us, having no idea how to meditate, spent gazing at the mesmerizing current as it carried the waters of the Mississippi toward the Gulf of Mexico. These were splendid, if not educational, times, at least until we had to return to our classroom. To do that, we had to climb the thirty feet up back up the bluff and walk that long stretch of even ground back to the Ford plant.

One October day, to celebrate the picture-perfect weather, we walked an especially long way before descending to river level. After a leisurely sojourn during which no yoga instructor training took place, we began the return trip. At first I felt fine, walking and talking with one of my classmates, but after a few minutes, I did not have enough breath to do both at the same time. My classmate was happy to walk silently beside me, but even then, I could not continue. I had to rest. By this time, we were well behind the rest of our group, so I asked her to go ahead without me, and I would follow in a few minutes. My handbag, which contained my rescue inhaler, was locked in our classroom, as was my cell phone, so my only recourse was to walk slowly and rest frequently. It took me an hour and a half to walk the half mile to our classroom, where, upon arrival, I ravenously inhaled Albuterol while my relieved classmates told me that at that very moment, our teacher was driving around searching for me. "Why hadn't she seen me?" I wondered.

The three best-known forms of embodied yoga are meditation (*pratyahara* in Sanskrit), breath control (*pranayama* in Sanskrit), and physical postures or poses (*asana* in Sanskrit). These practices are embedded in the culture that created them, so to fully understand them, you must understand the culture itself, including Sanskrit, the original language of yoga. In addition to embodied practices, yoga also includes a complex of philosophical and spiritual teachings that addresses habits of living, notions of the divine, and morality. But I was not interested in becoming a serious student of yoga. Had I wanted to make that commitment, I would have probably had to study in India, as the American teachers I most respected had done.

My goal was vocational. I knew how yoga's physical practices had helped me, and I wanted to use those practices to help others. Though I received my teaching certification, which was the credential I needed in order to be hired as a yoga teacher, my actual yoga education began in earnest after that, when I took more than a dozen online continuing education classes from the field's most respected teachers and attended in-person workshops taught by these same teachers when local yoga studios brought them to the Twin Cities as visiting instructors. Most critically, I learned from my students, whose physical behavior, facial expressions, and feedback taught me everything I needed to know in order to become a sensitive, compassionate yoga teacher.

*

From the moment I decided to become a yoga teacher, I had a clear vision. I wanted to teach older people an age-appropriate, body-sensitive approach to the physical practice of yoga in community-based, nonprofit settings so that I could serve people who would otherwise not have access to yoga. I called my approach Third Age Yoga, using a term coined by a twentieth-century British historian named Peter Laslett, who wrote a classic book on positive aging called *A Fresh Map of Life.* Laslett characterized life's first age as "growing up," its second age as "earning and parenting," and its fourth age as "true old age." His third age refers to an era after earning and parenting but before true old age, in which we continue to enjoy reasonably good health and well-being, and during which we remain engaged in the adventures of life, whatever those may be. The essential idea behind healthy longevity is to extend the third age for as long as possible, thus shortening the time spent in frail old age.

I began my Third Age Yoga practice by teaching free classes at a neighborhood public library. Once I had some experience, I applied to teach a yoga class at the West 7th Community Center, a small nonprofit organization near my downtown St. Paul neighborhood. West 7th meets urgent human needs working from a small space on a small budget, including monthly meat sales, assistance with home mainte-nance, nursing services, exercise and safety classes for older adults, and after-school programs for children and teens. St. Paul's smallest but most appreciated public library is also located in the center.

I made my pitch to Jeannie, the center's adult programs coordinator, and to my delight, she felt that there would be an enthusiastic audience for a gentle yoga class geared to mobile older people. We decided to charge six dollars per class per person. I would be paid four of the six dollars up to a maxi-mum of forty dollars per class, and we agreed to accept up to twelve participants. It took no time for the class to fill, and within the first three months, we were overfilling it. We opened wait lists, but we also knew that it was time to add another class. After the first year, we opened a third class for Third Age Yoga "alumni" who wanted to learn a wider variety of poses.

West 7th Community Center became my teaching home for the next eight years, even when I was also teaching at other community venues. Over that time, I worked with people who ranged in age from their early fifties to their middle eighties, but most of my students were in their middle to late sixties and early to middle seventies. I hasten to add that some of my oldest students were also some of the most capable. A majority of my students were women, but I also worked with many men, some of whom were the husbands of my female students. Most of my students were retired, but had worked as teachers, nurses, flight attendants, physicians, social service workers, homemakers, and at many other vital occupations.

Some were lifelong singletons, some were longtime divorcees, some were widows and widowers. They were kind to each other and to me, which put me at ease. They came to class with an assortment of physical challenges and singularities, all of which we addressed in good spirit with safe, appropriate adaptations of our practices. One of my youngest students, a woman in her late forties, was recovering from chronic fatigue syndrome when she came to Third Age Yoga. One of my most determined students, an energetic woman in her seventies, had had both shoulders replaced, and another, who was only in her fifties, had had both knees replaced.

Together, we weathered bad backs and pulled muscles, colds and flu, treatments and procedures, ice storms and snow days, and a gamut of milestone birthdays. Together, we experienced yoga as a healing practice that we could rely on to help us feel better. My students were open, willing, and trusting, and together we created a learning community of mutual respect, support, and tolerance. I felt honored to be invited into their social circles, and eventually I learned that even though we were diverse in many ways, we all held similar political convictions. I loved these exceptional people when they were my students, and I love them now.

Every student I taught (and there were several hundred over my nine-year teaching vocation) learned how to practice healthy skeletal alignment, both standing and seated, in order to avoid fatigue and minimize low back pain; how to safely and comfortably lower to the ground and rise up again, either with or without the help of a chair; how to balance on one foot; how to safely move into, hold still in, and move out of at least sixty yoga poses; and how to relax body and mind while sitting or lying still. I did not lecture on yoga philosophy or spirituality, nor did I pretend any knowledge I did not have. I was not teaching "authentic" yoga. I was teaching easily accessed, entirely secular yoga-based practices. Whenever I asked my new students why they had never tried yoga, the majority said they thought that it was at least partly a spiritual or religious discipline involving chanting and prayers.

The spiritual dimensions of yoga could not have been farther from my mind when I was hired to teach a weekly yoga class at the Wilder Community Center for Aging, a beautiful facility in one of St. Paul's oldest inner-city neighborhoods. Built and supported by the Wilder Foundation, a venerable service organization named for the wealthy St. Paul businessman whose fortune and generosity made it possible, the foundation plainly announces on its website that it is "Here for Good." Among its services, the center offers an adult day health program that "helps older adults with memory loss, mental health concerns, and physical or chronic conditions such as diabetes or heart disease to maintain their independence while experiencing meaningful connections, a sense of belonging, and an enhanced quality of life."

For nearly three years, I taught a diverse group of about a dozen special people who had been cleared by the center's nurses and physical therapists to participate in a yoga curriculum that I had specially designed to serve their unique needs. Each week, we gathered in a circle that was large enough for participants to stand behind their chairs and do a full range of standing yoga poses, including single-leg balances, wide-legged bends, twists, and lunges. Our classroom had a twenty-foot run of windows, under which was a countertop with a slight overhang. Almost every week we lined up at the counter, supporting ourselves by grasping the overhang, and did full-bodied yoga sun salutations, a sequence of poses traditionally done in the morning. When we reached the point in the salutation where we moved into the downward-facing dog pose, we barked, creating a hilarious cacophony of dog vocalizations.

Though some of their names have faded from my memory, my Wilder students themselves have not. I worked with several stroke survivors whose bodies were weaker on one side than the other, but yoga, with its attention to symmetry, helped them improve their stability. I also worked with several people who suffered from various forms of dementia but who loved yoga and had no trouble creating stable, graceful shapes with their bodies. My oldest student was Estella, who was ninety-eight when I worked with her. She had better balance than I did and was quicker of mind, too, making her a yoga teacher's dream student. Jack was a muscular man who one could see had been physically powerful earlier in his life but who suffered from severe arthritis when I worked with him.

His back was so bent forward that a physical therapy assistant had to belt himself to Jack while he practiced yoga, but after three or fourth months, Jack was able to stand perfectly upright behind his chair. The staff thought it was a miracle and arranged for a group of physical therapists, nurses, and physicians to visit our class and observe Jack and the other students.

Rosemary was living in the aftermath of a severe stroke and was taking medications that left her limp and sleepy (perhaps because she was overmedicated), but she came to class whenever the staff could wake her. She was a pale-skinned young woman with the rosiest cheeks I have ever seen, and she always wore a fancy straw hat with a plump ring of multi-colored flowers resting on its brim. Sometimes her hat was tipped to one side, and sometimes she wore a red shawl. Most weeks she fell asleep during class, but when we gently roused her, she would smile widely and sweetly as she opened her eyes. Sharon sometimes had trouble concentrating, sometimes she became agitated or moody, and sometimes she teased her best friend, Rosie, but yoga gave her a channel through which to focus her attention, so most of the time she was engaged and beautiful in her poses. She was enthusiastic, too, often calling out, "Let's do the dog!"

For my Wilder students, the most welcome part of yoga was the time we devoted to relaxation at the end of each class. We would sit in our circle, close our eyes, and in a gentle voice, I would guide the group in a body scan, a mental journey during which we briefly rested our attention on each part of our bodies in turn, from the tips of our toes to the tops of our heads. During the scan, I would encourage everyone to allow each part of their bodies to loosen and relax, especially

any places that felt uncomfortable, whether from a tight muscle, an upset stomach, or a restless mind.

More than any of my other yoga students, my Wilder group
loved this practice. Over the years, I have often wondered why.
For many of my other students, spending even five minutes
(let alone the ten we spent at Wilder) in an awake state of still-
ness verged on torture. Though they may have taken an hour
on a Tuesday morning to practice yoga, that may not have
been enough time to clear their minds of the everyday clutter
they carried to class and that awaited them when they left. My
Wilder students spent their entire day at the Center for Aging
participating in activities intended to engage their minds and
assuage their cares. Because of the circumstances of their lives
and beings, most of them did not carry the kind of mental clutter that accompanies most of the rest of us as we manage our
days. That burden was borne by their relatives and caregivers,
so perhaps their minds were more spacious than those of most
of my other students. Perhaps, after our physical practices,
they simply felt tired and wanted to relax, or perhaps they
were growing wings.

*

Helping is healing. I can attest to that. Now, a decade after
the fact, I can see that my decision to become a yoga teacher,
a path that, at first glance, seemed so far afield from the work
I had always done, was the catalyst that ultimately allowed
me to emerge from complicated grief. The basic human
instinct to do for others can, as experts have believed for
years, save the life of the helper as well as the helped. When
I was a young woman taking interest inventories designed to
clarify my career goals, I always scored lowest on "helping

professions." I was not, apparently, suited to nursing, social work, or human services. In fact, I now think that these kinds of surveys, which, like everything else in my earnest young life, I took much too seriously, were at least partly to blame for a skewed conception of myself as a person who cared not a fig for the welfare of others but preferred to create art, write, analyze, and wield influence over my fellow humans. Looking back through the long lens of fifty years, it is ironic that the "selfish" vocations I preferred were actually potent helping professions that allowed this nonhelper to serve others in meaningful ways for three decades.

No matter the catalyst, emerging from over a decade of acute, complicated grief is predicated on readiness. Moving to my glass-walled condominium helped me emerge from emotional and physical darkness into light. In a life-saving happenstance, having a fitness center under the same roof as my home motivated me to begin exercising regularly. Once my physical fitness had improved, I felt confident enough to take a yoga class. I cannot overemphasize the boost in well-being I felt from becoming a person who was willing to work diligently to improve her physical fitness and, after that, becoming a person who could master and practice an array of yoga poses. Lunching with my physician friend, Bill, and receiving, through him, the notion that I could actually become a yoga teacher, occurred only because my mind had opened enough to hear and heed that call.

No matter the reasons and no matter that they appear to form a succession of fortuitous coincidences, I had reached a point where my inner life had evolved enough so that I could look outward again. I could see a new place for myself in the earthly world. It was as though my grief had been displaced by yoga: there was, in the end, not enough space in my mind to feed my love of yoga while also tending to my timeworn grief. When I actually started teaching, I was overjoyed to see the good I was doing for others. As human beings, we act in ways that will benefit others sometime in the future, ways that we, ourselves, may never witness. Often we must take our good deeds on faith, but as a yoga teacher, it is as though you are watching a garden grow before your eyes. The fruits of my students' and my labors bloomed early and opened into sustained beauty. With them in mind, I could, as the Carter Family sang in 1928, keep on the sunny side.

11

A Close Brush with Death

TEN YEARS AND THREE MONTHS after Tom's death, at ten o'clock on the night of Tuesday, November 4, 2008, news outlets in the United States had just projected that having won a victory in Virginia, Barack Obama, the junior senator from Illinois, had won the presidential election. The numbers had been going his way since the earliest poll closings, and now it was certain. Suddenly, in a release of anxiety and a gush of profound hope, I was crying a roaring river of tears, and I could not stop. Nor did I want to stop. I was, for the first time in over a decade, overjoyed to be alive. I was lucky to be alive! I was grateful to be alive! As the grinning president-elect, his elegant wife, and his two adorable daughters took the stage at Chicago's Grant Park, the crowd of 240,000 supporters who had gathered to witness history burst into cheers that were heard around the world.

When he came to the microphone, the president-elect affirmed that "[This election is] the answer that led those who have been told for so long by so many to be cynical and fearful and doubtful of what we can achieve, to put their hands on the arc of history and bend it once more toward the hope of a better day." In that moment, I understood that the reason I had survived the past decade was so that I could witness this night. That Tom had not lived to do so did not diminish my joy. I thought of it: I wished hard that he had lived, but for the first time since his death, his physical absence was not a barrier to my happiness.

Such is the rapture of justice. It can relieve our grieving and restore our weakened souls. It can turn the tables. All my life, I had never understood how any person could treat another as if that other were not human. Skin color aside. Homeland aside. Profit aside. Vengeance aside. Nothing in the history books, nothing in the first-person narratives, nothing I had heard in school or in personal conversations, nothing I had ever known had explained why. As a Jewish child born in the closing weeks of World War II, I was taught early to "remember the six million." I learned what the Shoah was, but I never learned why, exactly, it had happened. As an adult, I read and read to learn why. Why slavery in a so-called democracy? Why the Holocaust? Why any form of dehumanization? I have never found a plausible answer, and in the light of three-quarters of a century gone in my life, I now see that is because there is none.

Nevertheless, I simply cannot believe that there are inherently bad people and inherently good people, and that these states of being are immutable because they are inherited. If we are born with healthy bodies, including our brains, I believe that each of us possesses nearly infinite capacity to act for the good of others while acting on behalf of our own happiness.

In truth, one probably cannot exist without the other: they are a double helix. Apart from mental illness, it is the circumstances of our lives that can turn us away from goodness, not the fact of being born. I am only now coming to see that in the years since Tom's death, no matter how many times I contemplated choosing death myself, no matter how pervasive my misery, no matter how thickly veiled any vision of the future appeared, I was, and probably always had been, a grudging optimist.

I now know that selling our home and buying my condominium were acts of optimism, not abandonment. My entirely unforeseen embrace of yoga, and my eagerness to help others using the energy I derived from it, were not only acts of optimism but the first deliberate initiatives I had taken since Tom's death to do some good in the world. Both these acts pushed against my grief. I had reached a point where consciously or not, I was at last resisting the sorrow that had smothered me for the longest ten years of my life.

Without realizing it, I had been moving from prolonged, acute grief to what I now understand as mourning, a process during which "bereaved people seek and find ways to turn the light on in the world again." Dr. M. Katherine Shear says that "when successful, mourning leads people to feel deeply connected to deceased loved ones while also able to imagine a satisfying future without them. After mourning successfully, a bereaved person is re-engaged in daily life, reconnected to others, and able to experience hope for a future with potential for joy and satisfaction." In deed if not in thought, I was moving toward President Obama's "hope of a better day." I had lived in grief for so long that when my feelings of sadness and longing began to ease, I was not aware that my emotional state was changing. As ten years turned to a dozen and then to fifteen, I was finally able to recognize that two of my long-felt states of being had transformed themselves: I did not miss Tom as intensely, and I was weary of feeling sorry for myself.

These milestones were not clear demarcations. I never had a conversation with myself in which I surmised that I was beginning to feel alive again. I did not awaken one sunny morning suddenly feeling more able to meet the world. It was a slow ascent, like traveling from St. Paul (elevation 795 feet) to Denver (elevation 5,280 feet), a rise of 4,485 feet spread over 917 miles. This ascent, which I have made many times, is decidedly slow, but not necessarily gradual. The transformation of topography from woodland to prairie to plains to foothills to mountains occurs in fits, starts, and plateaus, as do human transformations. I doubt that anyone travels a smooth, gradual road out of the depths of despair into the heights of happiness.

Still, time is distance. One of the reasons most Minnesotans love living here is nature's gift of seasonal variety. Summer is blooms, birds, breezes, and basking under the high sun; fall shades of yellow, orange, crimson, and pink offer a spectacular finale to the temperate seasons; the snows of winter lay down a calm white blanket that dazzles the eye under a shocking blue January sky; and the unfolding spring brings us all back to life as the earth is once again revealed and we feel the sun's warmth on our skin. In Minnesota, the seasons are one of the most obvious ways that nature marks time, but because time is distance, the change of seasons became my worst enemy soon after Tom's death.

On July 28, 1998, the day he died, summer reigned. Harbingers of fall were still weeks away, and I felt palpably, whisperingly close to him. Only a few days earlier I had seen his face, I had touched him, I had kissed him. In bed, he had wrapped his body around mine. Two weeks, then three, seemed less than a moment to me: I could still smell him; I could bury my nose in his dirty T-shirt and inhale him. It was summer, the last season of his life, and at least in my mind, it was easy for us to be together.

Then, September. I returned to my job. The weather began to cool. Still, I was visiting the cemetery every day, I was embracing Tom in my mind, I was sleeping with him in my mind, and I was talking aloud to him throughout my waking hours. But when the leaves turned yellow and the nights turned cold, my already intense pain abruptly intensified. It had been two months since I had last laid eyes on him. Summer was gone, and my first fall without him had arrived. Suddenly, those two months felt like an eternity. It was the turning of the season, an alteration that could not be denied as I looked out from our kitchen window at the scattered orange and yellow leaves lying in the backyard, that jolted me into the excruciating realization that the distance between us was lengthening, day by day, month by month, season by season. That pain was nearly unbearable and would only get worse as the first fall turned to the first winter and the first winter turned to the first spring and the first spring turned to the first summer.

As my separation from Tom grew longer, I began measuring it according to the cycle of seasons. Fall was the season of desperate longing, winter the season of ruthless sorrow, spring the season of fear and sickness, and summer the season of death. Each new season brought a grim reminder that there was no hope that Tom would return and a diminishing chance that I would relieve my pain by joining him. For a decade, the change of seasons buttressed my grief. Even fall and spring, the two most glorious seasons in Minnesota, made me feel wistful and forlorn. If one cannot feel uplifted by the miracles of nature, what hope is there?

What I came to learn is that, ironically, time itself can become the bearer of hope, if not strictly the healer of wounds. Time, I now believe, can overtake even complicated grief. When the seasons turned one into the other for the tenth or eleventh cycle since Tom's death, I no longer thought to perceive those changes as grievous milestones in my ever-lengthening separation from him. I began, unintentionally, to accept them simply and humbly for what they were: the manifestations of nature's cycles. I also began to appreciate each season as a sign of hope and a badge of survival. After all, even the advent of winter meant that the days would grow longer and lighter. No matter the other forces for good that had entered my life, time, by virtue of its passing, had gradually become the single most powerful force for my restoration.

*

To purchase my condominium, I had to take a mortgage, so I reluctantly gave up my plan to retire at sixty-two. Instead, with the approval of my dean, who welcomed the chance to save a few dollars, I reduced my University appointment to 70 percent time. I went to my office only three days each week, and that made it easier to manage my Crohn's symptoms, which, until my surgery, were still ruling my life. Though those symptoms were my immediate reason for seeking a reduced appointment, I never said that to my dean or anyone else at the University. I simply said that I had reached a point where I wanted to gradually phase into retirement, which was also true. My reduced appointment, along with the dean's genuine benevolence, also meant that I had to make fewer commutes in snowstorms, for me one of the most stressful parts of living and working in Minnesota. I worked 70 percent time for three years (until my sixty-fifth or "Medicare" birthday) and 50 percent time for two years until, elated, I left my office for the last time.

Retirement, including partial retirement, not only grants a gift of time, it is also a recipe for well-being. During my work with Encore Transitions, the program that helped people prepare for life after work, I learned that well-being, not the absence of disease or chronic conditions, is the most meaningful measure of health after midlife. For people like me, who have incurable but mostly manageable health conditions, high well-being is the cornerstone of a vital later life. High well-being not only helps us heal from our losses; it makes us more resilient during an era when we are sure to face some of life's most taxing exigencies. According to *Psychology Today*, well-being is characterized by "good mental health, high life satisfaction, and a sense of meaning." It is an outlook in which we recognize and resist what is bad in the world but are simultaneously buoyed by an abiding sense that life is good. Until I moved into my condo, more than nine years after Tom died, I was not able to feel the preference for life that defines well-being.

Some of the rarely discussed benefits of retirement are the very ones that can elevate well-being, including not having to set an alarm and rise before you have gotten enough sleep, not having to pack a lunch, not having to go to work sick, not having to go to work with a compromised immune system, not catching colds from colleagues who sneeze and cough all over you, not having to commute in a snowstorm, not having to travel from St. Paul to Duluth and back again in a fog so heavy you cannot see the hood of your car, not having to walk across a large campus in a driving rain wearing nylon stockings and pumps because you are on your way to meet with the university provost, not being frustrated by rush hour traffic, not having deadlines, not having to deal with "difficult" people, not having to interact with people you do not trust, not having to worry that you do not have access to a private bathroom, and not having to endure these stresses for thirty or more years. If you remove the word *not* from this list, all these situations undermine well-being.

On Wednesday, June 27, 2012, after five years of part-time work and thirty-four years at the University, I walked out of my office and into retirement. That day, I had parked on the roof of the Gortner Avenue parking ramp, and as I walked into the afternoon sun and toward my car, warming myself after my final day in my frigid office, I felt the deepest rush of bliss I had ever experienced. My work life was over.

It had begun at age nine when I started working as a cashier in my father's grocery store, and it was ending fifty-eight years later on a sun-washed rooftop overlooking the Minnesota state fairgrounds. In between, I had worked not only as a grocery store cashier but as an accounting clerk at a now-defunct local insurance company, as a computer programmer at the same company, as a fidelity and surety claims secretary at the Los Angeles office of Travelers Insurance (where one of the two male claims adjusters for whom I worked cried when I tendered my resignation), as a sales clerk in the record department of St. Paul's Emporium department store (where I purchased every Beatles album the day they arrived), as an exhibition installer at the University of Minnesota's Coffman Union art gallery, as an accounting clerk at Rosedale Chevrolet (where, after a customer paid cash for a car, I had to sort and count thirteen thousand dollars in coin and small bills out of a musty brown cardboard box), and as an accounting clerk at the Twin Cities office of Mutual of Omaha (known to its employees as the Wild Kingdom), where, in preparation for an outside audit and after two years of failed attempts by their staff, I managed to bring into balance the massive checking account from which the office paid insurance claims.

I had served a fifty-eight-year sentence, and now I was free. No more clock watching. No more night work. No more weekend work. No more travel. No more false politeness. No more having to go to work ill. It was an old saw come true. You know, the one about the employee who woke up one morning to the blazing realization that she could no longer stand her job. She called her supervisor to explain. "I quit. I've been sick the entire time I've worked here, but now I'm calling in well. Goodbye." By the time I left the University, I was commuting only two days each week, and I was, by choice, no longer part of my unit's operations and culture, so even after thirty-four years, I felt no sadness when I retired. Nor did I experience mixed emotions. I felt only joy.

At long last, I could manage my diseases! To teach a yoga class, I only had to be away from home for about ninety minutes, and if I had a cold or COPD exacerbation, I could cancel class. With the right medications, I was able to maintain a busy teaching schedule, at one point teaching five classes each week. Still, I knew that I would put my health at risk if I taught too many classes, so I looked for other ways to reach people who might benefit from my approach to yoga. I worked with

St. Paul's local nonprofit cable access network to produce two yoga videos designed for people who were homebound, and I self-financed a video in which I taught viewers how to safely lower to the ground and rise up again, either with or without the help of a chair. I even published an illustrated book on restoring flexibility through yoga.

Working with Third Age Yoga was a tonic for my soul, and no matter how I felt physically and emotionally, it buoyed me. If nothing else, I was living proof to my students that an older person with significant, even debilitating, diseases could safely practice a full range of yoga postures. I never experienced the loss of a sense of belonging that often accompanies the first months of retirement because by the time I left the University, I already belonged, heart and soul, to Third Age Yoga. To be able to devote my attention to just one pursuit was one of the greatest gifts of my retirement. Sometime during my sixties, I had lost my ability to "multitask," as had most of my friends and acquaintances. I could no longer comfortably juggle several simultaneous roles and projects, as I had done without question for the past three decades. I had also lost my ability to scan the landscape of my responsibilities in order to determine which areas most needed my attention, and I had lost my tolerance for "good enough." Now my time was my own, and so were my values.

*

The year was 2016. The month was May, the date was the twenty-sixth, the day was Thursday. The time was soon after noon. (My afternoon yoga class would begin at one thirty.) I was standing in the shower, rinsing away soap and shampoo, when I began to feel dizzy. Within what could only have

been three or four seconds, the dizziness had risen to a cre-
scendo, exploding into the sharpest, most brutal headache I
had ever experienced. The epicenter of this excruciating pain
was at the very top of my head: it felt as though someone
had dropped a rock on it. The dizziness continued; by now,
ten or twelve seconds had passed.

Calm down and get out.

I tried to talk to myself, to give myself instructions. I managed to turn off the water, step out of the bathtub without
losing my balance, and sit down, wet and naked, on the toilet.
By now, the epicenter of my headache was starting to diffuse.
The pain was losing some of its ferociousness, but the pressure
and heaviness had now spread throughout my head. I was
also nauseated and in the throes of a sudden case of diarrhea.
I resigned myself to the revolting prospect that if I were going
to vomit, it would have to land on the floor. After several
minutes of diarrhea, the nausea subsided, and the dizziness
seemed to be diminishing a little. The enveloping headache
continued unabated.

I managed to rise from the toilet. Somehow I dried myself
and pulled on my bathrobe. Though it took all my will, I managed to call West 7th Community Center and tell the staff that
I would not be able to make it to class. (I remember feeling
disembodied: distant from the person who made that call.) I
laid down on the sofa. After an hour or so, I forced myself to
get up, drink water, and take ibuprofen. Still, the dizziness and
headache hung on. I returned to the sofa, where I stayed until
about eight o'clock that night, when I got into bed. By then,
the dizziness had diminished, but my head still felt like it was
enclosed in a 360-degree vise. I could have mistaken it for an
overpowering sinus headache.

When I awoke the next morning, all that remained was a dull, heavy-headed fuzziness that felt like a hangover. I knew that I had experienced an unusually severe "episode," but I told myself that it must have been a colossal sinus attack (whatever that might be) or, more likely, Crohn's disease symptoms. After all, it was not uncommon for me to experience a headache, dizziness, nausea, and diarrhea all at the same time during a Crohn's flare-up. Luckily, the weekend was nigh, and I did not have to teach again until the following Tuesday. By then, the heavy-headedness had eased a little, but it refused to let go. I began to worry. I did not want to live with a permanent headache, even a muffled one, so I went to see my doctor. I told her about my episode. Could it have been caused by sinus congestion? Could it have been caused by Crohn's? She was unwilling to hazard any guesses. Instead, she sent me for an MRI of my head.

The day after the MRI, she called me. My sinuses looked clear, but there had been an "incidental finding:" a brain aneurysm. Oh, a brain aneurysm. A brain aneurysm? What? It was possible that I had read or heard that term, but I had no idea what a brain aneurysm actually was. And what was an "incidental finding"? Did it refer to something small and inconsequential? Or was it something that the reading physician noticed offhandedly while searching for the central cause of my headache? My doctor briefly explained what a brain aneurysm was, but because I can no longer remember what she said, I offer this definition from the Johns Hopkins Cerebrovascular Center:

> A brain aneurysm is a bulging, weakened area in the wall of a blood vessel in the brain, resulting in an abnormal widening

or ballooning of that vessel. An aneurysm may occur in any blood vessel, but is most often seen in an artery rather than a vein.

Though this description does not evoke a fruiting tree, most illustrations liken a brain aneurysm to a berry hanging from a branch, the branch representing the blood vessel from which the aneurysm sprouted. As the aneurysm fills with blood, its walls becomes thinner and thinner, like a balloon filling with air. If its walls become too thin, the aneurysm can leak or even rupture. My doctor was taking no chances: she sent me for a consultation with a neurosurgeon.

Dr. Eric Nussbaum, a neurosurgeon who happens to practice in the Twin Cities, is considered one of the world's leading specialists in the treatment of brain aneurysms. The National Brain Aneurysm and Tumor Center calls him "a national expert in the diagnosis and treatment of brain aneurysms and vascular malformations. He is among a small group of surgeons worldwide who specialize in microsurgery for brain aneurysms. He has performed more than 2,000 complex surgeries to treat brain aneurysms." Early in his career, he was regarded as a wunderkind, and even in midlife, he remains a renowned innovator, treating patients from all over the world. In a coincidence of fortune, I had hit the jackpot in my own hometown.

A good thing, too, because as Dr. Nussbaum told me during our consultation, my symptoms were "textbook" for what is called a "sentinel bleed." A sentinel bleed, he explained, is a leak from an aneurysm that is often a precursor to a rupture. A rupture occurs when an aneurysm bursts, spilling blood into surrounding tissue. About 40 percent of the time, a ruptured aneurysm causes death, and about 66 percent of the 60 percent who survive are left with "some kind of neurological deficit." Moreover, a rupture can sometimes lead to a hemorrhagic stroke, in which the patient "bleeds out" rapidly, usually within an hour. Dr. Nussbaum judged that there was more than a 50 percent chance that I had experienced a sentinel bleed, and recommended that I undergo surgery within the next few weeks. In the meantime, I needed to have an angiogram so that he could study the aneurysm in more detail.

Death? A hemorrhagic stroke, the very condition that had killed my ninety-year-old aunt three years earlier? A "neurological deficit?" And what about my long-anticipated vacation in New Mexico, scheduled for late July? I had a choice between believing that I was on the precipice of a quick but gory death or pretending that my leak was not sentinel and simply carrying on as though I were immortal. I asked Dr. Nussbaum whether he thought I could wait until early August to have surgery, explaining that I was hoping to take a vacation in late July. A man of few words and little flourish, he replied, "I don't see why you shouldn't." There I was, a walking slot machine: maybe I would pay and maybe I would not.

A week later, I reported to Regions Hospital for an angiogram, my sister Nan beside me. Angiograms allow physicians to create close-up, detailed images of abnormalities in our blood vessels. To begin the procedure, a tiny incision is made into an artery in the groin. (The groin, by the way, is the area between the lower abdomen and the thigh on either side of the pubic bone.) A thin tube, called a catheter, is then inserted into that artery. Mounted on the leading end of the tube is a tiny camera. The neurosurgeon guides the tube through the artery until it reaches the area to be examined (in this case, my brain aneurysm), and then navigates through it, capturing images as he or she goes along. Those images can then be used for diagnosis and as a guide while performing surgery.

After stripping entirely, I put on a hospital gown and was told to remove my glasses. Instead of packing them with my other belongings, I asked the nurse to give them to Nan. (If you are severely nearsighted, it is frightening to be separated from your glasses.) I was wheeled into an operating room, where, within seconds of my arrival, a gang of three men had gathered around me. One was slapping electrodes on my body (including under my gown), another was wrapping my head in a cap of some kind, and the third had lifted my gown so that my pubic area was exposed for all to see and was busily shaving my pubic hair.

"WAIT! HOLD ON! STOP!"

They froze. I pulled my gown down, covering my pubic area.

"Who are you? Why are you doing these things to me? Don't you dare lift my gown again! Have you no respect for human dignity?"

They backed away. The next thing I remember is seeing a female nurse smiling directly over my face and saying something like, "Doctor is here and we'll get started." At that point I lost consciousness, although I cannot remember being given an anesthetic. I woke up in a recovery room, where, to my utter surprise and burning rage, I was told that I had to lie flat on my back for four hours to assure that my incision had completely clotted. It was four hours of hell, and the only saving grace was that Nan patiently, blessedly, endured it with me. The most frustrating part of the whole ordeal was that no one was able to give me a logical explanation for my imprisonment. Why do I need to be flat on my back? Why four hours? Why not three? Or two? What would happen if I sat up? In the twenty-first century, in a large neurology unit in a large urban hospital, in the middle of the day in the middle of the week, no one knew.

Hospitals, I learned that day, can quickly transmute you into a sick person even if you are not sick. I entered as a (sort of) well person (except for my chronic diseases and a life-threatening brain aneurysm), and within an hour, I was immobile. I had to drink through a bent straw, I had to pee into a bedpan, my vital signs had to be monitored every thirty minutes, I was naked save for a pin-striped gown, I was wearing green paper slipper-socks on my feet, I had only crackers to eat, and if I had had to move my bowels, heaven only knows what would have happened. As if that were not enough, hospital stays can be contagious, as was the case with the abscess caused by the bacteria that entered my abdomen while my small intestine was resting on my stomach during my hemicolectomy. While granting all this, I must also note that hospitals can be places in which miracles are performed and people are snatched by the living from the cloying arms of the grim reaper.

The day after my angiogram, Dr. Nussbaum's assistant, Jody, called me. My surgery was scheduled for August 8, 2016, and incidentally, the angiogram had revealed that I actually had two aneurysms on the same blood vessel, one behind the other. Because of the way in which they were positioned, only one of them had been visible on my MRI. Jody explained that this was highly unusual. Equally unusual were the shapes of the aneurysms themselves, which Jody did not characterize. Brain aneurysms are commonly treated in two ways: coiling, in which thin metal wires are wrapped around the aneurysm, creating a mesh casing that prevents the aneurysm from growing, leaking, or rupturing; and clipping, in which a metal clip is placed at the base of the aneurysm to cut off its blood supply, thus preventing it from growing. Unlike clipping, coiling is usually accomplished through noninvasive endovascular surgery. A catheter is inserted into an artery in the groin, and using tiny tools mounted on the leading end of the catheter, the surgeon performs the coiling procedure.

Because of the peculiar characteristics of my aneurysms, only one of them could be treated with coiling. The other had to be clipped, which meant that I would need to undergo a craniotomy. An incision would be made in my scalp, a piece of my skull (called a bone flap) would be removed so that the aneurysms would be visible and accessible, one aneurysm would be coiled, the other would be clipped, and the bone flap would be returned to its proper place and covered with a titanium plate that would be screwed to my skull. I would need to spend four or five nights at United Hospital, located half a mile from my home.

*

Armed with doxycycline and prednisone so that I could breathe well enough to slowly make my way in the thin mountain air of Santa Fe, I went on vacation. I had promised myself that I would not worry about my brain aneurysm until the day of my surgery, a resolution that was easy to keep while basking in the "land of enchantment." In the 1990s, Tom and I had twice traveled to New Mexico and Arizona during summer road trips. I had also studied contemporary Native American arts and artists of that area as part of my doctoral studies, even bringing several of those artists to teach at Split Rock. After my colon surgery, travel became easier for me, and for the past six summers I had vacationed in Albuquerque and Santa Fe, making day trips to nearby pueblos to meet artists, learn about their work, and purchase their artwork as my budget allowed.

While in Santa Fe, my home was the legendary La Fonda Hotel, in which one feels like a grateful extra in a 1930s movie while lounging in the iconic lobby, strolling down the art-lined hallways, peeking into the gem shop or bootery, or stopping for a conversation with the concierge. Eating scrumptious blue-corn piñon pancakes each morning at La Plazuela, the hotel's sunlit dining room walled with hundreds of hand-painted glass tiles, made me feel as though I were dining in heaven on the food of the gods. Even when dining alone, as I almost always did, I felt no trace of self-pity in that exquisite environment.

*

At seven thirty on the morning of Monday, August 8, 2016, Nan and I reported to United Hospital, St. Paul's largest. I arrived bathed, sans breakfast, and ready to get it over with, whatever "it" turned out to be. The previous day, I had had a call from Dr. Nussbaum's office to say that my surgery, which had been scheduled for nine thirty, would now take place two hours earlier because Dr. Nussbaum had ordered another angiogram immediately prior to surgery in order to get current images of my aneurysms.

Two cheery nurses "prepped" me. I was naked under my hospital gown, but instead of paper socks, the nurses outfit-ted me with thick, fuzzy hospital slippers that would keep my toes toasty while I was "on the table." The operating room nurses, both women, came to introduce themselves and answer my questions. (I can no longer recall whether I asked any questions, but given my fear that I would lose my glasses forever, I am sure I must have asked where they would be stored. If I was lucky enough to awaken from surgery, I knew that I would need them immediately.) The anesthesiologist visited, assuring me that in spite of my emphysema, and even though I would be breathing through a tube, I should come through surgery no worse for the wear. He said they would have "emergency breathing equipment" at the ready, but that was only a precaution. Jody, Dr. Nussbaum's assistant, also came to visit. She told us that the surgery should take about two hours, and that Dr. Nussbaum would speak to my family as soon as I was "off the table." Finally, Dr. Nussbaum visited, reassuring us that my aneurysms were fully treatable and I had nothing to worry about.

With all due speed, a person (whose gender or role I cannot remember) arrived to wheel me to the operating room, along with a "patient relations" staff person who must have been affiliated with Dr. Nussbaum's office because I remembered meeting her when I had my angiogram. Here was my chance to try to right an inexcusable wrong. Gently but urgently, I told her about my degrading experience with the three ignorant, thoughtless (and sexist, but I did not say that) male staff people who had "worked on me" in a humiliating way without my permission (or for that matter, without any talk at all, not even hello) when I arrived in the operating room for my angiogram. I suggested that in the few minutes we had together while I waited to be taken for surgery, we should talk about how to prevent this from happening again. I implored her to institute two standard protocols in the treatment of female patients: protection of physical privacy and preservation of human dignity. All patients, and especially women being treated by men, require these two basic humanitarian acts from both male and female caregivers. She nodded in agreement, taking notes as we talked. We ended our conversation with her promise to work to try to improve this behavior.

I was wheeled into the operating room, where the two nurses I had met during my prep welcomed me. The room was bright, almost cheerful, and I remember looking up, as a functionally blind person might, at their fuzzy, smiling faces. After that, I remember nothing of the surgery or the operating room. I know that I was taken to the recovery area after surgery, but I have no memory of that, either. When I awoke, at (what I think was) about four in the afternoon, I was in a large private room in the intensive care unit. I was breathing oxygen through a cannula, I was wearing electrodes attached to a heart monitor, and I was receiving fluid and antibiotics intravenously. I remember that my siblings were sitting in a wide, ragged ring around my bed, anxious to tell me what Dr. Nussbaum had told them, but I was still groggy from the anesthesia, and I kept drifting in and out of sleep, and I remember none of what they said. The next morning, my sisters gave me a report.

Dr. Nussbaum had come to talk with them at about two o'clock, immediately after finishing my surgery. He said that the procedures had taken about an hour and forty-five minutes and had gone according to plan. There had been no setbacks or surprises, and he expected me to make a full recovery. When they asked about my breathing, he said I did "great." Still, they had remained in the family waiting room until I was transferred from recovery to my room in the ICU. They wanted to see with their own eyes that I was breathing comfortably and still in my right mind. Jody also visited them to corroborate Dr. Nussbaum's report and answer their questions, partly, I am sure, because Dr. Nussbaum is a man of so few words. Even now I do not know the full details of my surgery. I do know that my incision began in the middle of my forehead at my hairline, went straight back for an inch or so before it turned left and traveled across my head to my left temple and down the left side of my head, ending at my hairline just in front of my left ear. I can easily trace it with my finger: the contours of my post-incision scalp bring to mind the dry river beds, gullies, and ridges on the surface of Mars.

By the morning after surgery, I was awake enough to realize that I had no headache and only a little soreness along my incision. The beauty of brain surgery is that it does not interfere with the organic operations of one's body, so my digestive tract was not affected. Breakfast time! I ordered dry whole wheat toast, orange juice, fresh fruit, and coffee from the hospital's bountiful menu. Everything sounded delicious, so I was not expecting the disparaging disparity between the descriptions of the food on the menu and the actual food I was served: soggy toast, mushy cantaloupe, watery orange juice, and cold coffee. Thank goodness Nan answered my emergency call for a bran muffin and hot coffee. Unfortunately, breakfast was only the tip of the inedibility iceberg. It turned out that the only hospital food I could tolerate was the chicken noodle soup, which I ate noon and night for my entire stay.

After breakfast, I quickly discovered that it was business as usual in the ICU. First, the "hospitalist" on duty paid me a visit. I will call him Dr. Yes. A fun-loving neurologist who would follow my progress for my full stay, he seemed surprised but delighted at my alertness. Earlier, during my first trip to the bathroom, I caught a look at myself in the mirror, and what I saw shocked me. My head was completely encased in a white gauze bandage that had been rolled around my head several times so that it looked like a cross between a turban and a chef's hat sans the ballooning top. My left eye and cheek, as well as my neck, were a deep shade of plum. My forehead was mustard yellow. Add my oxygen cannula and glasses, which were both askew, and I looked like a drunken short order cook who had just come out on the short end of a bad street fight. Upon seeing me, Dr. Yes remarked that if anyone should ask me what had happened, I should simply reply, "You should see the other guy!"

Dr. Yes said that two nights is the standard ICU stay for craniotomy patients who are recovering without difficulty. That meant that the next morning, if all was well, I would be moved into a private room in the neurology unit. After I had spent one night in the neurology unit, we would discuss when I could go home. I would be required to pass several tests before I could leave the hospital: I needed to be free of infection; I needed to be able to care for myself at home, which Dr. Yes deemed critical because I lived alone; my incision needed to show evidence of healing; and I needed to be neurologically stable, which meant that my muscles had to be innervating normally and I had to be able to (convince Dr. Yes that I could) think clearly.

Shortly after Dr. Yes left, Jody looked in on me. She, too, seemed delighted with my condition, but wanted to make absolutely certain that my recovery went smoothly. She spoke clearly and firmly about what I could and could not do during my convalescence. First and foremost, I could not bend over for forty-five days, which, in practical terms, meant no yoga. When I told her that I was scheduled to return to teaching in early October, she made a face, saying that October might be optimistic and I should consider waiting until November. She also told me that while she did not expect me to have much pain, my greatest challenge during recuperation would be fatigue. She cautioned me to be patient. "The recovery is gradual," she said, "and you won't be able to rush it." At that moment, I was so elated to have cheated death that I cared little about how long it might take me to recover.

Nan arrived with my bran muffin and coffee. I was eating voraciously when another visitor arrived, an occupational therapist who had come to teach me how to live alone without bending over. Not only was she surprised by how alert I seemed, she was downright astonished by how easily I could walk unassisted. She plainly had expected to encounter someone in some unknown state of disability, if not complete immobility. During my adventures in the medical community, I have seen this repeatedly. Young people, even trained health care professionals, too often imagine people in their sixties and seventies as frail of body and feeble of mind, so when an older person of average vitality presents herself, they are shocked.

The therapist was amazed by how steady I was on my feet, how well I could balance, and how upright I could stand. Knowing that I was not allowed to bend over, she posed a problem: "Your sock is on the floor. How will you pick it up?" Instead of bending from the waist, I squatted, which kept my back and head straight. She was delighted. At that point, I laughingly revealed to her that I had been practicing yoga for more than eight years, and that, in fact, I taught yoga to older people. All that she admired—my stability, my posture, my balance, my agility—I attributed to yoga. My physical abilities were typical of yoga practitioners my age, I explained, while suggesting that she consider including certain yoga practices as part of her occupational therapy repertoire. Even Dr. Yes wholeheartedly agreed that it was the physical fitness I had acquired through yoga that had warranted my release from the hospital after three, rather than four, nights.

On Thursday, August 11, 2016, I went home, bruised and tired, but profoundly relieved. As the nurse had instructed, I took a shower without getting my head wet while Nan stood watch over me just outside the shower. It took all my energy, but I managed without incident. I felt confident that I could take care of myself without assistance. I would not be allowed to drive for two weeks, so it was my sisters, whom I could not live without, who saw to my groceries and other necessities. Over the next few days, I learned exactly how accurate Jody's cautions about fatigue had been. It took everything I had to lift myself up from the sofa and move, whether to use the bathroom, get a drink of water, or put together a rudimentary supper. For the next several weeks, my main occupations would be watching campaign news on MSNBC, reading when I was alert enough, and ruminating in the free psychological space created by activity restrictions.

For the first time since I had been diagnosed with a probable sentinel bleed, I let myself reflect on the weighty fact that I had had a close brush with death, my second since Tom died. Over the past eighteen years I had become a master at closeting disturbing thoughts, but now I genuinely wanted to try to make sense of what had happened to me. Since my first meeting with Dr. Nussbaum, I had refused to consider that my aneurysms would rupture before my surgery date or that I would die during or soon after surgery. I, who had longed for death for a decade; I, who had been apathetic toward life for even longer; I, who, after all that longing and apathy, had finally gotten a chance to walk through heaven's gate, had somehow survived, not by choice, but by chance.

I now knew that I was more likely than the average person to experience a lethal brain aneurysm rupture, and I knew that I had incurable diseases that would shorten my lifespan. How would I carry on? For nearly two decades, I had known without articulation how sad and disappointed Tom would have been to see me enduring such prolonged misery. Now, having faced both a grief-driven death wish and a fait accompli in the form of a close encounter with a killer aneurysm rupture, had I, once and for all, become a person who genuinely wanted to live? Given that I was still alive, what would I do with my remaining time and energy? My time on Earth might be short, and I might never regain the physical energy I took for granted before my health challenges had taken their toll. What of personal importance had I postponed? What had I mistakenly abandoned?

I was not able to return to my yoga classes until early November, and even then, the two weekly classes I was teaching completely drained me. By the end of the year, I had decided to teach only one class each week. That enabled me to continue with my longtime students at West 7th, but at the same time, I knew that my teaching practice was coming to an end. I no longer felt excited about continuing my yoga education and deepening my practice, which meant that I would no longer be able to offer my students new techniques and approaches. The irreversible truth was that my body could no longer support my teaching. To my surprise, it was an inevitability I could accept with gratitude because by the time I recovered from brain surgery, my heart had set itself on a different path, one that led home.

12

For the Sake of My Soul

I HAVE ALWAYS BEEN AN ARTIST. I cannot remember not being an artist because there was never a time in my life when I was not an artist. There were times when I did not make art, but even in those times, I was still an artist. I think of myself as an artist in the same way that I think of myself as a girl who grew into a woman, a Jew, a brown-eyed white person, a Gilats. Art has always been the breath of my life, even when I consciously turned away from it. Art is my beating heart, and when, after seventy-one years, everything else had been cleared away or used up or otherwise finished, it was all I had left and all I wanted, and it was not used up or finished. It was waiting for my return.

For too much of my adult life, I had kept my love of painting in a rubble-ridden hovel in the back of my mind. Here is what I told myself. Painting was self-indulgent: I should be helping others. Any painting of mine would make no contribution to the welfare of humanity: I should be helping others.

I was not talented enough to justify spending my time painting: I should be helping others. I was too tired to paint. I was too depressed to paint. I did not have time to paint. I did not know what I wanted to paint. I was never satisfied with my paintings. Art school had taught me that I should not begin painting until I had made preparatory sketches, but drawing made me anxious because it was so difficult to get it right. Failure does not build character, it eats away at it.

How far I had traveled, I thought, from those excuses. How far I had come from such pointless fears. Now, as I lounged in the newly vacated spaces in my mind, all those messages seemed meaningless, weightless. In my extended state of rest, I could not hang on to them; they dissipated. There were no distractions, no obligations, no unfulfilled duties. Now there was nothing for me to do but paint. I knew it: I could feel it in my hands. The compulsion to knit or paint or draw or write had always begun in my hands, and now I could feel it every day as I looked at my hands and rubbed them together. It had been four years since I finished my paintings of Townes Van Zandt and Frank Zappa, two of my favorite musicians in heaven, but long absences from painting had never seemed to dissuade me. In fact, they were a hallmark of my adult life.

Until I started art school in my middle twenties, I never experienced self-doubt about my artistic inclinations. I simply took my hobby for granted, creating whatever I wanted whenever I wanted however I wanted. My parents, seeing how much I loved to make pictures, kept me supplied with finger paints, crayons, paper, watercolors, and chalk. For my sixth birthday, they gifted me with the giant Jon Gnagy Art Studio in a Box, which I consumed as though it were caramel corn. When I was ten, I was allowed to use money I had saved from working at my father's grocery store to purchase a three-legged easel at the Ben Franklin variety store in Highland Village, our neighborhood shopping center. I used that easel until I was about fourteen, when I started painting with oils. To support my deepening commitment, I went to Ben Franklin and bought an adult-sized A-frame easel. I took no art classes, and I never had private art lessons. I simply drew and painted, experimenting as I went along.

I attended high school during the height of the Cold War, so, guided by my guidance counselor, who had been guided by my standardized test scores, I was placed in math, science, and foreign language classes. Though it makes me cringe to say so, art classes were usually reserved for students who were not "college bound," and my challenging "college prep" class schedule left no room for them. This is precisely how, early in life, we begin to be separated from our heart's desires. I had chosen Spanish as my foreign language, and, with encouragement from Mrs. Fleming, the kindest teacher I had ever known, I completed a four-year curriculum in three years. It only made sense, then, that I would enter the University of Minnesota as a Spanish major with the fantastical intention of someday living somewhere in South America (perhaps the Argentinian pampas) and working as a translator.

Unfortunately, however, my father's grocery store had gone bankrupt, leaving him unemployed. Even though I was working part-time as a grocery store cashier at Del Farm Supermarket, I could not afford to stay in college. In the spring of my sophomore year, I dropped out, leaving unpaid tuition and incomplete courses in my wake. I had to make a living, so I got a job at an insurance company as an accounting clerk. My ten years of experience operating a cash register had prepared me well for spending my days with my eyes on a spread sheet and my fingers on a calculator, so I was hired at a salary of $270 per month, twenty dollars more than the advertised pay. At twenty years old, I was working full time, I was painting when I felt like it, and above all, I was partying, which, in the long run, proved to be my most prescient occupation in the summer of 1965.

One June evening, my friend Sherry and I went to a party at a friend of a friend's home in Minneapolis. There we met a crowd of kids with whom we had not previously been acquainted. One of them was a beautiful blue-eyed blond boy named Tom Dayton. He was the cutest boy I had ever seen: tall, well-built, wholesomely handsome with a turned-up nose and an endearing overbite. Most remarkable was his charming way of easily and naturally articulating his feelings. His unexpectedly soft, modulated voice matched his manner perfectly: I remember having to strain at times to hear him over the party din. Tom was utterly masculine, yet the way he communicated could only be characterized as feminine. We talked all evening, discovering that we enjoyed the same kinds of music, that we had both graduated from St. Paul's Central High School, that for the first five years of my life we had lived two blocks from each other on Laurel Avenue, that even though he was born in 1946 and I was born in 1945, our birthdays were only five days apart, and that having enlisted in the United States Navy some weeks ago, he was scheduled to report for basic training the following morning.

What rotten luck! My disappointment must have been palpable because immediately after his confession, he asked if he could write to me, and would I write to him? He promised to write as soon as he knew his mailing address. I gave him my address and telephone number, but even as I handed him the scrap of paper, I was sure it was an exercise in futility. The best boy I had ever met, and now he was off to the navy and he would never write and I would never see him again and I would have to recover from one more broken dream. But a week later I had a letter, the first of a dozen he would write during his eight weeks in basic training. We covered the gamut of our interests and feelings during our correspondence, and by the time he returned home for a two-week leave, we were in love.

We had two dates and then I heard nothing from him. I counted the days that had elapsed since I had last seen him, trying to figure out when he would leave to return to the navy. He returned, I assumed, to the navy, and still I heard nothing from him. Summer was ending, fall was beginning, and I heard nothing from him. I gave up hope. Finally, after what must have been six weeks of silence, a letter arrived. He was in school, training to be a jet mechanic. He was sorry that he had not called or seen me, and he was sorry that on the night we met, he was too afraid to mention that he had a longtime sweetheart, his steady girlfriend throughout high school and beyond. He loved me, but he had made a promise to her that he was bound to keep.

It was more than I expected: at least he had made an attempt at honesty; at least he bothered to tell me. I never replied, and he never wrote again. In one of the greatest regrets of my life, I tore up his letters and threw them away. I went on with my job at the insurance company, I attended the weddings of my high school friends, I drew, I painted, I read the best-selling books of the day. Sometime between 1965, when I met Tom, and 1970, when the now-legendary

Hungry Mind bookstore opened in St. Paul, I began reading the early texts of the modern feminist movement: *The Second Sex*, by Simone de Beauvoir; *The Feminine Mystique*, by Betty Friedan; *The Female Eunuch*, by Germaine Greer; and *How to Make It in a Man's World*, by Letty Cottin Pogrebin. ("You do not have to be the secretary," Pogrebin writes, "you can be the boss!") These writers described the conversion to feminism as a sudden apprehension: a light bulb turning on in the mind. So it was in my life. One day I was an intellectually curious young woman with a broken heart, and the next I was a feminist, a part of my identity that would strengthen me for the rest of my life.

I was now a woman who made her own decisions, and I had decided to return to college. I now knew that any further formal education I undertook had to be for the sake of my soul, so I signed up for a drawing class at the Minneapolis College of Art and Design (MCAD). After just one session with MCAD's most illustrious drawing teacher, Paul Olson, I knew I was home. Under Paul's patient guidance, I spent two years learning how to draw. When I enrolled at the University of Minnesota in hopes of earning a bachelor's degree in fine art, I had already acquired the foundational visual skills that I later discovered were not taught in the University's art department.

At the time I entered art school, the University's drawing and painting faculty was dominated by a group of abstract expressionists who had cut their artistic teeth in post–World War II New York City, making them witnesses to, if not full participants in, the emergence of the New York School. What led them to Minnesota, I will never know, but I assume it was the need for a steady income. Here, outside their milieu, they could pretend to be big men on campus, sometimes arriving at class inebriated, sometimes manipulating the bodies of nude female models, sometimes giving graduate critiques in nearby bars, sometimes assigning grades without remembering which student's work was which. Once I understood the lay of that land, I studied exclusively with the department's younger generation of teachers, who, while working abstractly themselves, tolerated aesthetic diversity among their students.

There was one notable exception to this all-male faculty, a visiting professor named Mary Abbott, who taught at the University of Minnesota for ten years without academic rank or tenure. She was my watercolor teacher, but at the time I knew her, I did not realize that she was a major figure in the abstract expressionist movement of the 1950s. Nor did I know that she was as well known for her extended love affair with the artist Willem de Kooning as she was for her paintings. How I regret not approaching her to learn more about her development as an artist, the challenges she faced as she navigated New York City's sexist art culture, and how she had sustained her artistic identity into her fifties, when she came to Minnesota. At least now, more than forty years later, I can note that I admire her life and work, and I can now see magnificence in her paintings. Mary Abbott passed away on August 23, 2019, at the age of ninety-eight.

I was painting my way to a college degree, but while doing that, I was also pursuing an independent education in feminist art, an exploding contemporary movement about which, I am sorry to say, my University teachers, except perhaps Mary, knew nothing. Led by the artists Miriam Schapiro and Judy Chicago, I was discovering art made by women who were embracing traditionally feminine subjects, from household interiors to pattern-based images inspired by lace and embroidery. As new journals and books were published, I was reading the history of women artists as it was being written by a new generation of feminist critics and scholars, including my art history heroes, Linda Nochlin (*Why Have There Been No Great Women Artists?*) and Lucy Lippard (*From the Center*).

By the time I graduated in 1977, I had an aesthetic allegiance, but no money. I wanted to continue painting, so I worked a series of temporary jobs for nearly a year before I conceded that in order to live an independent life, I needed a full-time job. I began applying for jobs at the University of Minnesota, hoping to find work that had at least a tangential relationship to the arts. I held firm on that desire, and finally, in late August 1978, I interviewed for a secretarial job in a department called Continuing Education in the Arts. About two hours after the interview, I received a telephone call offering me the job. I accepted, and the rest became my history.

Coincidentally, that same evening my mother called to tell me that I had had a phone call from a young man who wanted to get in touch with me. "He was a nice, soft-spoken fellow named Tom Dayton. He said he was an old friend of yours, so I gave him your phone number. By the way, he asked if you were married. I said no, she's single, and he was elated. He said, 'That's wonderful!'"

The next evening he called me. We got reacquainted. He had been divorced from his high school sweetheart for several months, and his only son was living with her. He had never stopped thinking of me, and he was hoping I might be willing to get together. By any chance, would I like to go to the Minnesota State Fair with him that weekend?

"You bet!"

We went to the fair together (where I got nauseated from drinking beer on an empty stomach), and from that evening on, we were never apart. Tom explained that even when he had been happy in his marriage, he had continued to have feelings for me, and he hoped, if I could find it in my heart, to earn my forgiveness for having hurt me thirteen years earlier. We began cultivating in earnest the love that had blossomed so long ago, and we grew as close to each other as two people can. Shortly after Tom died, my cousin Scott, who lived two houses up the block from us, told me that he had never seen two people so much in love.

*

A new year had just arrived, my physical energy was gradually increasing, and after four months of postcraniotomy ruminating on the sofa, I now knew what I wanted to paint and how I wanted to paint it. For thirty years, I had been collecting Native American art by contemporary artists. I had a large collection of beadwork, and I had accumulated a small but beloved collection of Hopi kachina dolls and clay figures made by Pueblo artists. I especially loved my small sculptures of "mudhead" clowns, characterized by their spherical eyes, ears, mouths, and topknots, and "storytellers," which depicted mothers and their babies in stunning diversity. Each year, during my annual trip to New Mexico, I stretched my budget in order to acquire a few artworks that I felt I could not live without. It filled my heart with joy to meet the artists who made these exquisite objects, learn the histories and cultural contexts of these art forms, and have these artworks in my home so that I could feel uplifted by their beauty every day of my life. For years, I had wondered how I could share my love of these breathtaking objects, and now I knew: I would paint them.

Ever since art school, I had eschewed making unreadable paintings: unfocused, haphazard abstract compositions that offered no apparent meaning other than as an artifact of the painter's process. I wanted clarity. As someone who had recently escaped the grim reaper, I could no longer afford to spend months on one painting, and I was tired of complexity for its own sake. I wanted intimacy and simplicity. I was tired of "hidden" meaning too. For heaven's sake, if you could not see it in the painting itself, how would you know it was there? I wanted engagement, connection. I was tired of visual tricks and technical facility. I wanted honest, straightforward pictures that would honor their subjects. Above all, I wanted to feel joy as I painted. I longed to recapture the innocent pleasure I had felt as a child artist.

Unfortunately, after forty-two years of use and abuse, my easel had become so wobbly I could no longer use it. That, too, I dismantled and, piece by piece, discarded. I bought a new one on sale, which Nan and I put together one long afternoon using seven pages of opaque instructions written by a good Samaritan English teacher in New England. I had always enjoyed making my own canvases because it was an exercise in optimism: assembling stretcher bars to create a frame, stretching canvas over that frame using a pliers designed for that purpose, and priming each canvas using gesso, a mixture of paint and glue. Even ordinary activities, when done in an optimistic frame of mind, can take one on a flight of delight, and indeed, I felt like a cheerful songbird as I busied myself preparing canvases while listening to Bob Dylan's *Nashville Skyline*.

I knew that for my first painting, I would make a picture of an extraordinary clay sculpture that had been custom-made for me. A mudhead storyteller, it combined the two types of figures I loved best in one beautifully conceived and executed piece. It depicts a sitting grandmother holding a baby in each arm and a decorated pot between her calves. Each baby is holding a baby of her own, making the two babies mothers themselves. All told, the piece features five figures of generationally decreasing size. The topknots, ears, eyes, and noses of each figure, while circular in shape, are disks rather than spheres, giving the family an outlandish look that is typical of the witty tradition of mudhead clowns.

I came by this astonishing piece while vacationing in New Mexico. For years, I had known that Jemez Pueblo, about fifty miles northwest of Albuquerque, was a hotbed of artistic activity. Colleagues had told me that some Jemez artists opened their homes to visitors, so in 2013, I decided to visit. As I drove along the pueblo's main road, I saw a sign that said Open House with an arrow pointing east, so I turned onto a tiny road that served as a driveway to several homes. On the screen door of one of them was a sign that said Open, so I parked the car and approached the house. Waiting behind the door was Felicia Fragua, who welcomed me into her living room and introduced me to her sister, Chrislyn Fragua. To the right of the door, there was a glass display case containing about two dozen clay pots and sculptures, and ahead was a large living and dining room with a huge wooden table at one end. I was invited to take a seat at the table, where Felicia was hand-coiling a pot and Chrislyn was shelling peas. Every nerve in my body was at attention: I had entered art lover's heaven.

Until that day, I had not known Felicia's art by sight. I had not realized that at that very moment, there were, on a shelf in my den, a tiny storyteller by Felicia and a captivating open-mouthed frog by Chrislyn. I had not known that Felicia's large pots had won awards and were in demand by collectors. I only knew what I saw that day—that she was gifted. Creating in clay was like breathing to her. As we talked, I learned that Chrislyn and Felicia were part of one of Jemez's largest, most renowned art families. They were both full-time artists who sold their work mostly through galleries and museum shops, but also at seasonal markets. They had been taught by their mother, grandmother, and aunts, and both had been working clay since they were little girls. I asked Felicia what kinds of pieces she most enjoyed making, pots or storytellers?

"Both, of course!" she replied with a shy smile, and then, "Why don't I make you a mudhead storyteller with a pot?"

"I would love that!" I exclaimed. We negotiated a price, and I paid half of it as a down payment. I encouraged Felicia not to worry about whether I would like the piece, but to use her creativity in whatever ways made her happy. They asked where I was bound, and I told them I was planning to drive north and east through the Jemez Mountains to Santa Fe. "Do you have a gun?" Chrislyn asked, and when I said no, she matter-of-factly said, "Go back out to the highway and go home the way you came." The sisters gave me a generous bag of homemade cookies, there were hugs all around, and I went on my way. I never asked whether the gun would be needed against mountain lions or men: I was so relieved to have been warned that I felt giddy.

Three or four weeks later, Felicia called me to let me know that my pot was ready and she would be sending it the next

day. I assured her that as soon as I got it, I would send her
a check. Several days later, the package came. Needless to
say, I was euphoric. Beauty is one thing, technical mastery
is another, but unbridled creativity is bliss. Here was living
proof that indebtedness to cultural tradition does not pre-
clude originality. Now, more than three years after receiving
it, I was going to paint my most sincere interpretation of this
spectacular artwork.

I sketched my subject directly onto the canvas and started
painting. It was pure pleasure, and I got lost in it. The colors were few and the shapes were clear, but the background,
which featured elements of a remembered New Mexico landscape under a pink sky, did not suit the painting. Who cared?
I could simply repaint it! Imagine awakening each morning
knowing that you can spend your day engrossed in a creative
activity that envelops you in pleasure, lifts your spirit skyward, and entices you to put your troubles in perspective or
put them aside altogether. I had probably asked this of art all
my life, and now it was answering me at a time when, after
two decades, my grief seemed to be resting comfortably in the
recesses of my mind.

More paintings followed, and over the next year and a
half, I painted seventeen small canvases, each portraying one
or more kachina dolls, storytellers, or other clay figures. Several months into my painting project, it occurred to me that it
might be valuable to exhibit my paintings alongside the original artworks that had inspired them. By doing that, and by
including historical and cultural information about the Native
American pieces on exhibit, I could curate an art experience
for Native and non-Native viewers that would be educational
as well as visually engaging. I applied and was accepted for an

exhibit at the University of Minnesota's largest student-run art gallery, located in Coffman Memorial Union in the heart of the University's bustling Minneapolis campus. It was, in fact, the same gallery at which I had worked as an exhibit installer when I was in art school over forty years earlier. Life, indeed, is round.

After half a century of self-doubt, I had finally discovered a way to contribute something of value through my painting. Now that I had found my way back to the pastime that had afforded me such pleasure as a child, I realized that the work my art could do in the world, especially what might be learned from it, was as essential to me as the pleasure I derived from painting itself. It was possible, I realized, to unite my love of painting with my devotion to learning. I had dedicated most of my adult life to helping others learn, and there was no reason that my retirement from the University should bring that commitment to an abrupt, artificial end. I did not need an affiliation with an educational institution, nor did I have to surrender my identity as an artist in order to be an educator. If there is such a thing as a second (or third) wind, I had gotten it. It is never too late to build on one's past in order to break new ground in the future, even if you, yourself, are no longer unbroken.

In November 2018, my first solo show in forty-one years opened with a festive reception, where I was overjoyed to welcome family, friends, and colleagues, some of whom I had not seen since my retirement from the University. It was a heartwarming occasion marking a fitting completion of a project that had brought me more pleasure than I had thought possible in a life like mine. There was, of course, one person missing, the person whose happiness in the occasion would have been deepest, the person who would have been proudest of the artist, the person who would have been moved to tears on seeing his wife's accomplishment. After twenty years, there remained a hole in my heart that I knew would never fully heal, a fact to which I had resigned myself. I lived with that acceptance just as I lived with my ambivalent, perhaps impermanent, acceptance of the fact that I had lived.

13

Reconciliation

AFTER TOM'S FUNERAL, the funeral home, then called Hodroff and Sons, gave me a *shiva* candle. Encased in a six-inch-high royal blue glass cylinder featuring a white Star of David on its wall, the candle would burn for seven days. *Shiva,* a mispronunciation of *shevah,* translates to English as "seven" and is the Hebrew name for the first week of Jewish mourning, during which members of the deceased's immediate family receive visits from friends and relatives. If, during the visits, a *minyan,* or quorum, of ten post–Bar Mitzvah Jewish males is present, the Jewish mourner's *kaddish,* a prayer exalting God, is recited in Hebrew. This tradition is called "sitting *shiva,*" since its purpose is to provide sympathetic company to the bereaved. Because Tom was not Jewish, I was not obligated to sit *shiva,* but for each of the seven evenings following his funeral, I recited the mourner's *kaddish* in front of our kitchen stove, where his candle burned.

As guests arrived at Tom's funeral, they were given small cards that showed the mourner's *kaddish* in Hebrew alongside its English transliteration, so that those who could not read the Hebrew alphabet could say *kaddish* by reading the transliteration. I have never known the entire mourner's *kaddish* by heart, but I have heard it spoken enough times, and I have spoken it myself enough times, so that I can pronounce its words correctly when reading it. As a child, I spoke it in temple every *shabbat* as I stood beside my grandfather, and as an adult, I spoke it after the deaths of my grandparents. That is how, over five decades, the mourner's *kaddish* became imprinted on my memory, and it is also how the sadness associated with it became embedded in my soul.

Yit-ga-dal v'yit-ka-dash sh'mei ra-ba. These first words of the mourner's *kaddish* never fail to bring tears to my eyes. The fact that I no longer remember their meaning is beside the point; it is their long connotation with death and grieving that reawakens all my sorrows and forces them to surface. It is impossible for me to speak the mourner's *kaddish* dispassionately because it is fraught with a pervasive, cosmic sense of abandonment and aloneness that is more profound than the sadness I might feel as I remember any one person I have lost, including Tom. By speaking the mourner's *kaddish* each year on the anniversary dates of the deaths of their lost loved ones, Jews mourn again and again and again.

On the day of Tom's funeral, I also received from Hodroff and Sons a printed list of the annual anniversary dates of his death, called *yahrzeit* dates in Yiddish. There were twenty of them, beginning with 1999 and ending with 2018. Because they are translations of dates in the Jewish calendar, which is lunar, these anniversaries did not fall on the anniversary of his death according to the Gregorian calendar, but on nearby dates. Each *yahrzeit* date is different, but is nonetheless exactly one Hebrew year from the previous *yahrzeit*. On these dates, I honor Tom's soul by lighting a slow-burning *yahrzeit* candle in his memory and saying *kaddish* for him. About twenty-four hours later, the candle burns itself out, just as the *shiva* candle did after those seven *shiva* days so long ago.

After I lit my twentieth *yahrzeit* candle in 2018, I downloaded from a Jewish funeral home's website fifteen more years of *yahrzeit* dates, which will take me to 2033, when I will be eighty-nine years old, and Tom, as ever, will be fifty-two. I also continue to light annual *yahrzeit* candles for my mother and father, who, had they lived until 2020, would be 101 and 104, respectively. I do these things not because I still suffer from complicated grief but because I am the product of a religious heritage whose mourning traditions encourage ruminating, dwelling, and worshipping. By this I mean ruminating on the past and forever shaking one's head in disbelief, dwelling on the past and forever asking why, and worshipping the past so that one never fully recovers from loss but proceeds in time alongside it.

*

While *yahrzeit* is observed once a year for the rest of a Jewish survivor's life, if one has lost a parent or, in contemporary Judaism, a spouse or child, that practice does not begin until the second year of mourning. That is because after *shiva*, the bereaved survivor is obligated to recite the mourner's *kaddish* every morning for the first year after a loved one's death, a tradition called *shnat ha-evel*. Since Jewish law dictates that one is not supposed to recite the mourner's *kaddish* unless a *minyan* is present, as a practical matter, the survivor must go to synagogue every morning in order to say *kaddish* in the presence of a *minyan*. At the close of *shnat ha-evel*, the first *yahrzeit* is observed.

After Tom died, instead of dragging myself to temple early every morning to say *kaddish*, I went to Fort Snelling National Cemetery to visit his grave almost every day for two years. Unlike *shnat ha-evel*, my purpose was not to honor his ascending soul but to be as physically close to him as possible. During the first few months after his death, when the days were long, the weather was warm, and I was unbearably disconsolate, this daily ritual, which usually took place in late afternoon or early evening, was the only respite I knew. I kept a towel in my car, which I laid atop his grave and sat on during my sojourns. I often ate an early supper on his grave, either a plain McDonald's hamburger with a small order of French fries or two Taco Bell tacos. Oddly, I was able to digest these meals more easily than those I ate at home alone.

By late in the day, the area around Tom's gravesite was usually deserted, and I would talk freely to him as I ate, updating him on local activities: how many graves had been dug that day, new burials, new headstones, whether deer had been feeding on the flowers left at nearby graves, the ages, service branches, and military ranks of those buried nearby. There was life at the cemetery, and that is what occupied our attention. Most interesting to me was a man, middle-aged and silent, whom I often saw visiting a grave near Tom's. He always brought a lawn chair with him, and he would sit contemplatively in it for fifteen or twenty minutes. Then he would stand up, fold his lawn chair, and leave as quietly as he had arrived. Finally, after seeing him a dozen times, I walked over to read the headstone for the grave he visited. I can no longer remember the deceased's name, but engraved on the stone were the words WIFE AND MOTHER. Around the stone, he had draped a sparkly metallic banner, probably bought from one of the vendors who occasionally sold memorial goods outside the cemetery, that said LOVE YOU MOTHER.

When it rained or when it was too cold to sit comfortably outside, I stayed in my car, talking to Tom in the same way as I did when sitting on his grave. Sometimes, on those days, I would stand for a few minutes in front of his headstone. Sometimes, I would try to calculate the distance between my body and his, which I usually estimated to be three or four feet. Once, I even asked a passing groundskeeper how far underground the vaults enclosing the caskets were sunk. When winter came and the snow was too deep to navigate, my daily visit would be a slow drive-by, but when spring came around and the ground dried out, I gratefully resumed my outdoor visits. I maintained this ritual for about two years, until I began to tire of visiting every day. Many days, I felt too tired after a day of work to visit, other days I was unwilling to brave the weather, and still other days I rationalized that I could be with Tom at home, rather than at his grave.

Gradually, my cemetery visits became fewer and farther between. I visited on his birthday and, eighteen days after that, on the anniversary of his death. I visited on Veterans Day, but the cemetery was so crowded and the traffic near it so snarled, that after a few years, I stopped trying to visit that day. Memorial Day was a similar story. By and by, I stopped visiting on his birthday, and only visited on July 28 of each year. On the last of those anniversary visits, about ten years after Tom's death, something unexpected happened to me while sitting on his grave. Suddenly, I could not bear to be there. It hurt too much. I cried, but not tears of grief and not the benign, even welcome, tears of reminiscence, which I was still not capable of shedding.

I hurt because I was remembering—no, actually feeling—the depth of my pain in the first months and years after his death. There at his grave, those excruciating days abruptly flooded my consciousness. It was a roiling waterfall, and it refused to recede. I was reliving pain that was so unbearable, it shocked and scared me even after a decade.

Even though this inexplicable incident happened at a time when I felt myself emerging from prolonged grief, I would not characterize it as a relapse. Nonetheless, it was enough to end my annual visits to the cemetery. Tom's grave no longer felt like a sanctuary; suddenly, it felt like a cruel mnemonic. Though I am no longer afraid to visit the cemetery, I have not challenged myself to do so. But I still think of his grave, especially his headstone. Having been exposed to the elements for over twenty-one years, it is now, I am sure, well weathered, waiting for the day, a few days after my death, when cemetery workers will remove it and send it to a stone carver, who will engrave HIS WIFE on its blank side. It will then be returned to its home, where the two people buried beneath it will be resting in peace.

*

More than two decades after Tom's death, I am mostly, but not entirely, free from the debilitating cacophony of emotions I experienced while suffering from complicated grief. I no longer feel, as Katherine Shear says, "persistent yearning or longing for the person who has died," nor do I have "a recurring desire to die in order to be reunited with that person." I still believe that my "loved one is really gone forever." I cannot claim that I no longer have "inappropriately intense reactions to memories of the person who has died," it is just that I have gotten used to living in the company of those memories. I feel more peaceful, more settled, and while

I no longer wish to die, I am no longer afraid of dying, either. Still, even though more than twenty years have passed, I have not lost my desire to be reunited with Tom. The fact that I am still alive must mean that somewhere along the way, without consciousness or intention, I must have decided to live, and I remain at peace with that decision.

The positive psychology researcher Sonja Lyubomirsky defines happiness as "the experience of joy, contentment, or positive well-being, combined with a sense that one's life is good, meaningful, and worthwhile." These days, I often feel joy, my health is stable enough so that I feel a reassuring sense of well-being, and I continue to seek goodness while living in an often incomprehensible world. But I have never again experienced the everyday happiness I felt during my twenty-year marriage. Once Tom died, I never resumed the proverbial search for happiness that we are taught is the goal of life, the belief that tomorrow will be better than today even if today was satisfactory, that somehow, if we try, our lives will evolve in ways that will, once and for all, content us. Perhaps this is true, but I have given up on yearning.

Today, I live a settled life on the fringes of happiness. I have never recovered from losing Tom. Instead, I have reconciled myself to my loss so that I can live in relative serenity. Even though some experts tell us that recovery from grief should be our goal, I believe that for some of us, including me, reconciliation may be the only achievable outcome. Today, I am on friendlier terms with my loss, a relationship that I know will endure as I continue to age. But because my grief has never fully resolved itself, I am not able to feel unequivocal contentment, something to which I have also reconciled myself.

I will always wonder whether complete contentment is

possible if you do not have a living life partner whom you love first and most deeply among all the other people you love, and who loves you first and most deeply among all the other people he or she loves. I can imagine, but have not myself felt, that some people feel most free, most liberated, if their lives are not bound to a significant other, but I do not believe that kind of freedom is preferable to committed, mutual love. When two people love each other in kind and in measure, when each has the other's welfare first in mind, and when each can express and sustain a commitment to the other, happiness surely follows, at least it did for me. I believe this truth deepens as we age.

I wish that Tom and I had been able to grow old together. Still, that he lived for fifty-two years, that he was the lovable, loving person he was, and that I was given the chance to know and love him for twenty years brings as much grace to my life now as when he was alive. As Tom once said about his first wife, "You never stop loving the people you love." There is no better blessing than loving and being loved by a life partner, no matter the time or distance between the lovers' planes of existence.

Rather than consciously working to avoid my most painful memories, today I am able to allow myself a new pleasure: daydreams. Every so often, I enjoy picturing Tom as a healthy man in his seventies: retired, relaxed, perhaps wearing glasses, perhaps with a receding head of gray or white hair, perhaps with a bit of a paunch, observing life on the busy street below us, walking leisurely along the river bank, noting the water birds, tugboats, and barges as he strolls, or sitting on a park bench, content to watch river life drift by. I sometimes imagine that he has taken up snowshoeing or that he serves on our building association's beautification committee. Other times, I imagine the two of us walking to our favorite restaurant, nameless in my daydream, for a casual dinner out.

These fancies are occasional, brief, and agreeable. They reassure me that I can think of Tom without pain even though my most painful memories continue to survive in the deeper reaches of my mind, where they will only die when I do. Because they are pleasant, my reveries keep Tom close to me; I no longer feel apprehensive or distressed at the thought of leaving him behind. For me, daydreams are exercises in reconciliation. Some might say that such imaginings are unhealthy, that perhaps they indicate a more benign form of complicated grief. Some might say that in these moments, I am fleeing reality, but nothing could be farther from the truth. I do not believe that grief passes into the past. Instead, I believe, as the grief counselor Thomas Moore said, that it becomes a fixed element of character. The one for whom I grieve has not faded into inaccessibility. On the contrary, my memories of half a century ago are as vivid, as tactile, as the rose-red velour robe that warms me as I write.

I can taste Tom Dayton; he is on the tip of my tongue. I can remember every pore on his face, each nail on his fingers and toes, his face in profile as he opens his mouth to take a bite of toast, the precise color of his blue eyes. I can remember his voice in my ear, beside me in bed, over the telephone, from across the room, from another room, from his sickbed. I can remember the freckle on his right forearm that matches the one on mine, the shape of the hairs on each of his eyebrows, the way he whistled, the way he sang birdsongs, his question when, under hospice care, he was prescribed the antidepressant Zoloft: "When do I take off?"

ACKNOWLEDGMENTS

I WANT TO THANK MY SISTERS, Judy Gilats, Resa Gilats, and Nancy Levine, and my brother-in-law, Allen Levine, for their unwavering support in everything I do, including reading and offering their thoughts about *After Effects*. Nancy and Allen generously read several versions of the manuscript, and Allen introduced me and my memoir to Douglas Armato, director of the University of Minnesota Press, which allowed this book to find its way into the world. My deepest thanks.

I also thank three longtime women friends, all brilliant septuagenarians and octogenarians, for reading early versions of *After Effects* (so early that the book was then titled "Intense and Prolonged") and commenting honestly and thoroughly on them. Throughout my writing, revising, and rewriting, I referred to their incisive, indispensable notes. Thank you, Donna Bennett, Phyllis Campbell, and Carolyn Holbrook.

Two classic books guided me as I tried to write truthfully and ethically about living with and beyond complicated grief: *Writing the Memoir: From Truth to Art* (Eighth Mountain Press, 1997, 2002) by Judith Barrington and *Writing as a Way of Healing* (Harper San Francisco, 1999) by the late Louise DeSalvo. I have read these two books a dozen times over the past twenty years, and they were at my side throughout my work on *After Effects*. Because I had highlighted so many passages in them over the years, I had trouble choosing which to cite here, but in each book, one central idea served as a lighthouse during my writing journey. Barrington believes that meaningful memoirs consist of three essential elements: scenes, summaries, and "musings." She says that "rather than simply telling a story from her life, the memoirist both tells the story and muses upon it, trying to unravel what it means in the light of her current knowledge" (20). DeSalvo offers a related idea as she frames writing as a healing practice. "To improve health," she says, "we must write detailed accounts linking feelings with events. The more writing succeeds as narrative—by being detailed, organized, compelling, vivid, lucid—the more health and emotional benefits are derived from the writing" (22). Three pages later, she restates this in one salient sentence: "We must write in a way that links detailed descriptions of what happened with feelings—then and now—about what happened." Thank you, Judith Barrington and Louise DeSalvo.

Laurie Harper, longtime literary agent, publishing consultant at Author Biz Consulting, and counselor extraordinaire, was instrumental in helping me ready *After Effects* for publication. Thank you, Laurie. I treasure your insights and honesty.

I have been blessed to have Erik Anderson, regional trade editor at the University of Minnesota Press, as my editor. I have deeply appreciated his unique insights, the superb quality of his thinking, his gentle patience, and his dedication to

After Effects. Erik, I am forever grateful to you. My deepest thanks, also, to Paula Dragosh, for her masterful, respectful copyediting. Paula, thank you for bringing *After Effects* to a beautifully polished completion. Thank you, Judy Gilats, gifted book designer and beloved sister, for designing the book's pages. They are exquisite.

Finally, I want to acknowledge the only two books that genuinely consoled me during my first year of widowhood. Though I read, or tried to read, what I remember as a plethora of books about grief during that time, especially books by widows, only these two, both written by widowers, have stayed with me. The first is *Without* (Houghton Mifflin, 1998), the poet Donald Hall's collection of elegiac poems written after the untimely death of his wife, the poet Jane Kenyon, who died of leukemia in 1995 at the age of forty-seven. These bare poetic reports take the reader through the final stages of Kenyon's illness and then through the early stages of Hall's grief after her passing. The second book is *A Grief Observed* (originally published in 1961 and reissued by Harper San Francisco in 1994), the writer, theologian, and literary scholar C. S. Lewis's classic journal of grief written in the weeks following the death of his wife, the poet Joy Davidman, from breast cancer. This short but unsparing collection of excerpts from the notebooks that Lewis filled during this time is both a wrenching portrait of abject grief and an urgent account of the crisis of faith to which his unrelenting sorrow led. I heartily recommend both books to anyone who is humbled by the raw power of straightforward language, whether poetry or prose, to express human suffering. Books like these bring meaning to our lives at times when we most need to feel that we are not alone.

BIBLIOGRAPHY

Benjamin, Walter. *Illuminations: Essays and Reflections.* New York: Schocken Books, 1969.

Hyde, Lewis. *The Gift: Imagination and the Erotic Life of Property.* New York: Vintage Books, 1979.

Karnes, Barbara. "Gone from My Sight: The Dying Experience." Vancouver, Wash.: Barbara Karnes Books, 1986.

Laslett, Peter. *A Fresh Map of Life: The Emergence of the Third Age.* Cambridge, Mass.: Harvard University Press, 1991.

Lyubomirsky, Sonja. *The How of Happiness,* quoted in "What Is Happiness?" at the Greater Good Science Center, University of California, Berkeley. greatergood.berkeley .edu.

Neruda, Pablo. "Childhood and Poetry," quoted in Lewis Hyde, *The Gift: Imagination and the Erotic Life of Property.* New York: Vintage Books, 1979.

O'Connor, M. F., et al. "Craving Love? Complicated Grief Activates Brain's Reward Center." *NeuroImage* 42 (2008): 969–72.

Robinaugh, Donald J., and Christine Mauro, Eric Bul, Lauren Stone, Riva Shah, Yuanjia Wang, Natalia A. Skritskaya, Charles F. Reynolds, Sidney Zisook, Mary-Frances O'Connor, Katherine Shear, and Naomi M. Simon. "Yearning and Its Measurement in Complicated Grief." *Journal of Loss and Trauma* 21, no. 5 (2016): 410–20.

Shear, M. Katherine, et al. "Grief and Mourning Gone Awry: Pathway and Course of Complicated Grief." *Dialogues in Clinical Neuroscience* 14, no. 2 (2012): 119–28.

ANDREA GILATS is a writer, educator, artist, and former yoga teacher. She was the cofounder and longtime director of the University of Minnesota's Split Rock Arts Program, a nationally renowned series of residential workshops in visual art and creative writing, and Split Rock Online Mentoring for Writers, in which writers worked individually with master teachers. She is the author of *Restoring Flexibility: A Gentle Yoga-Based Practice to Increase Mobility at Any Age* and has written many essays and articles about aging. A grateful survivor of the coronavirus pandemic, she is writing a memoir about approaching old age during that dangerous time.